CHIANG KAI-SHEK

CHIANG KAI-SHEK

Sean Dolan

CHELSEA HOUSE PUBLISHERS

NEW YORK

NEW HAVEN   PHILADELPHIA

Chelsea House Publishers
EDITOR-IN-CHIEF: Nancy Toff
EXECUTIVE EDITOR: Remmel T. Nunn
MANAGING EDITOR: Karyn Gullen Browne
COPY CHIEF: Juliann Barbato
PICTURE EDITOR: Adrian G. Allen
ART DIRECTOR: Giannella Garrett
MANUFACTURING MANAGER: Gerald Levine

World Leaders—Past & Present
SENIOR EDITOR:: John W. Selfridge

Staff for CHIANG KAI-SHEK
COPY EDITOR: Terrance Dolan
DEPUTY COPY CHIEF: Ellen Scordato
EDITORIAL ASSISTANT: Marie Claire Cebrián
PICTURE RESEARCHERS: Karen Herman, Linda Peer
DESIGNER: Ghila Krajzman
PRODUCTION COORDINATOR: Joseph Romano
COVER ILLUSTRATION: James Tennison

First Printing

1 3 5 7 9 8 6 4 2

Library of Congress Cataloging in Publication Data

Dolan, Sean.
Chiang Kai-shek.

p. cm. — (World leaders past & present)
Bibliography: p.
Includes index.
   Summary: A biography of the longtime Chinese political and military
leader who established his government in Taiwan when the Communists
took control of China in 1949.
ISBN 0-87754-517-0

1. Chiang, Kai-shek, 1887–1975—Juvenile literature.
2. China—Presidents—Biography—Juvenile literature.
3. Taiwan—Presidents—Biography—Juvenile literature.
[1. Chiang, Kai-shek, 1887–1975. 2. China—Presidents.]
I. Title. II. Series.
DS777.488.C5D65   1988
951.04′2′0924—dc19   88-4299
[B]   CIP
[92]   AC

Contents

John Adams
John Quincy Adams
Konrad Adenauer
Alexander the Great
Salvador Allende
Marc Antony
Corazon Aquino
Yasir Arafat
King Arthur
Hafez al-Assad
Kemal Atatürk
Attila
Clement Attlee
Augustus Caesar
Menachem Begin
David Ben-Gurion
Otto von Bismarck
Léon Blum
Simon Bolívar
Cesare Borgia
Willy Brandt
Leonid Brezhnev
Julius Caesar
John Calvin
Jimmy Carter
Fidel Castro
Catherine the Great
Charlemagne
Chiang Kai-Shek
Winston Churchill
Georges Clemenceau
Cleopatra
Constantine the Great
Hernán Cortés
Oliver Cromwell
Georges-Jacques
    Danton
Jefferson Davis
Moshe Dayan
Charles de Gaulle
Eamon De Valera
Eugene Debs
Deng Xiaoping
Benjamin Disraeli
Alexander Dubček
François & Jean-Claude
    Duvalier
Dwight Eisenhower
Eleanor of Aquitaine
Elizabeth i
Faisal
Ferdinand & Isabella
Francisco Franco
Benjamin Franklin

Frederick the Great
Indira Gandhi
Mohandas Gandhi
Giuseppe Garibaldi
Amin & Bashir Gemayel
Genghis Khan
William Gladstone
Mikhail Gorbachev
Ulysses S. Grant
Ernesto "Che" Guevara
Tenzin Gyatso
Alexander Hamilton
Dag Hammarskjöld
Henry viii
Henry of Navarre
Paul von Hindenburg
Hirohito
Adolf Hitler
Ho Chi Minh
King Hussein
Ivan the Terrible
Andrew Jackson
James i
Wojciech Jaruzelski
Thomas Jefferson
Joan of Arc
Pope John xxiii
Pope John Paul ii
Lyndon Johnson
Benito Juárez
John Kennedy
Robert Kennedy
Jomo Kenyatta
Ayatollah Khomeini
Nikita Khrushchev
Kim Il Sung
Martin Luther King, Jr.
Henry Kissinger
Kublai Khan
Lafayette
Robert E. Lee
Vladimir Lenin
Abraham Lincoln
David Lloyd George
Louis xiv
Martin Luther
Judas Maccabeus
James Madison
Nelson & Winnie
    Mandela
Mao Zedong
Ferdinand Marcos
George Marshall

Mary, Queen of Scots
Tomáš Masaryk
Golda Meir
Klemens von Metternich
James Monroe
Hosni Mubarak
Robert Mugabe
Benito Mussolini
Napoléon Bonaparte
Gamal Abdel Nasser
Jawaharlal Nehru
Nero
Nicholas II
Richard Nixon
Kwame Nkrumah
Daniel Ortega
Mohammed Reza Pahlavi
Thomas Paine
Charles Stewart
    Parnell
Pericles
Juan Perón
Peter the Great
Pol Pot
Muammar el-Qaddafi
Ronald Reagan
Cardinal Richelieu
Maximilien Robespierre
Eleanor Roosevelt
Franklin Roosevelt
Theodore Roosevelt
Anwar Sadat
Haile Selassie
Prince Sihanouk
Jan Smuts
Joseph Stalin
Sukarno
Sun Yat-sen
Tamerlane
Mother Teresa
Margaret Thatcher
Josip Broz Tito
Toussaint L'Ouverture
Leon Trotsky
Pierre Trudeau
Harry Truman
Queen Victoria
Lech Walesa
George Washington
Chaim Weizmann
Woodrow Wilson
Xerxes
Emiliano Zapata
Zhou Enlai

CHELSEA HOUSE PUBLISHERS

ON LEADERSHIP

Arthur M. Schlesinger, jr.

LEADERSHIP, it may be said, is really what makes the world go round. Love no doubt smooths the passage; but love is a private transaction between consenting adults. Leadership is a public transaction with history. The idea of leadership affirms the capacity of individuals to move, inspire, and mobilize masses of people so that they act together in pursuit of an end. Sometimes leadership serves good purposes, sometimes bad; but whether the end is benign or evil, great leaders are those men and women who leave their personal stamp on history.

Now, the very concept of leadership implies the proposition that individuals can make a difference. This proposition has never been universally accepted. From classical times to the present day, eminent thinkers have regarded individuals as no more than the agents and pawns of larger forces, whether the gods and goddesses of the ancient world or, in the modern era, race, class, nation, the dialectic, the will of the people, the spirit of the times, history itself. Against such forces, the individual dwindles into insignificance.

So contends the thesis of historical determinism. Tolstoy's great novel *War and Peace* offers a famous statement of the case. Why, Tolstoy asked, did millions of men in the Napoleonic Wars, denying their human feelings and their common sense, move back and forth across Europe slaughtering their fellows? "The war," Tolstoy answered, "was bound to happen simply because it was bound to happen." All prior history predetermined it. As for leaders, they, Tolstoy said, "are but the labels that serve to give a name to an end and, like labels, they have the least possible connection with the event." The greater the leader, "the more conspicuous the inevitability and the predestination of every act he commits." The leader, said Tolstoy, is "the slave of history."

Determinism takes many forms. Marxism is the determinism of class. Nazism the determinism of race. But the idea of men and women as the slaves of history runs athwart the deepest human instincts. Rigid determinism abolishes the idea of human freedom—

the assumption of free choice that underlies every move we make, every word we speak, every thought we think. It abolishes the idea of human responsibility, since it is manifestly unfair to reward or punish people for actions that are by definition beyond their control. No one can live consistently by any deterministic creed. The Marxist states prove this themselves by their extreme susceptibility to the cult of leadership.

More than that, history refutes the idea that individuals make no difference. In December 1931 a British politician crossing Park Avenue in New York City between 76th and 77th Streets around 10:30 P.M. looked in the wrong direction and was knocked down by an automobile—a moment, he later recalled, of a man aghast, a world aglare: "I do not understand why I was not broken like an eggshell or squashed like a gooseberry." Fourteen months later an American politician, sitting in an open car in Miami, Florida, was fired on by an assassin; the man beside him was hit. Those who believe that individuals make no difference to history might well ponder whether the next two decades would have been the same had Mario Constasino's car killed Winston Churchill in 1931 and Giuseppe Zangara's bullet killed Franklin Roosevelt in 1933. Suppose, in addition, that Adolf Hitler had been killed in the street fighting during the Munich *Putsch* of 1923 and that Lenin had died of typhus during World War I. What would the 20th century be like now?

For better or for worse, individuals do make a difference. "The notion that a people can run itself and its affairs anonymously," wrote the philosopher William James, "is now well known to be the silliest of absurdities. Mankind does nothing save through initiatives on the part of inventors, great or small, and imitation by the rest of us—these are the sole factors in human progress. Individuals of genius show the way, and set the patterns, which common people then adopt and follow."

Leadership, James suggests, means leadership in thought as well as in action. In the long run, leaders in thought may well make the greater difference to the world. But, as Woodrow Wilson once said, "Those only are leaders of men, in the general eye, who lead in action. . . . It is at their hands that new thought gets its translation into the crude language of deeds." Leaders in thought often invent in solitude and obscurity, leaving to later generations the tasks of imitation. Leaders in action—the leaders portrayed in this series—have to be effective in their own time.

And they cannot be effective by themselves. They must act in response to the rhythms of their age. Their genius must be adapted, in a phrase of William James's, "to the receptivities of the moment." Leaders are useless without followers. "There goes the mob," said the French politician hearing a clamor in the streets. "I am their leader. I must follow them." Great leaders turn the inchoate emotions of the mob to purposes of their own. They seize on the opportunities of their time, the hopes, fears, frustrations, crises, potentialities. They succeed when events have prepared the way for them, when the community is awaiting to be aroused, when they can provide the clarifying and organizing ideas. Leadership ignites the circuit between the individual and the mass and thereby alters history.

It may alter history for better or for worse. Leaders have been responsible for the most extravagant follies and most monstrous crimes that have beset suffering humanity. They have also been vital in such gains as humanity has made in individual freedom, religious and racial tolerance, social justice, and respect for human rights.

There is no sure way to tell in advance who is going to lead for good and who for evil. But a glance at the gallery of men and women in *World Leaders—Past and Present* suggests some useful tests.

One test is this: Do leaders lead by force or by persuasion? By command or by consent? Through most of history leadership was exercised by the divine right of authority. The duty of followers was to defer and to obey. "Theirs not to reason why / Theirs but to do and die." On occasion, as with the so-called enlightened despots of the 18th century in Europe, absolutist leadership was animated by humane purposes. More often, absolutism nourished the passion for domination, land, gold, and conquest and resulted in tyranny.

The great revolution of modern times has been the revolution of equality. The idea that all people should be equal in their legal condition has undermined the old structure of authority, hierarchy, and deference. The revolution of equality has had two contrary effects on the nature of leadership. For equality, as Alexis de Tocqueville pointed out in his great study *Democracy in America*, might mean equality in servitude as well as equality in freedom.

"I know of only two methods of establishing equality in the political world," Tocqueville wrote. "Rights must be given to every citizen, or none at all to anyone . . . save one, who is the master of all." There was no middle ground "between the sovereignty of all and the absolute power of one man." In his astonishing prediction of 20th-century totalitarian dictatorship, Tocqueville explained how the revolution of equality could lead to the *"Führerprinzip"* and more terrible absolutism than the world had ever known.

But when rights are given to every citizen and the sovereignty of all is established, the problem of leadership takes a new form, becomes more exacting than ever before. It is easy to issue commands and enforce them by the rope and the stake, the concentration camp and the *gulag.* It is much harder to use argument and achievement to overcome opposition and win consent. The Founding Fathers of the United States understood the difficulty. They believed that history had given them the opportunity to decide, as Alexander Hamilton wrote in the first Federalist Paper, whether men are indeed capable of basing government on "reflection and choice, or whether they are forever destined to depend . . . on accident and force."

Government by reflection and choice called for a new style of leadership and a new quality of followership. It required leaders to be responsive to popular concerns, and it required followers to be active and informed participants in the process. Democracy does not eliminate emotion from politics; sometimes it fosters demagoguery; but it is confident that, as the greatest of democratic leaders put it, you cannot fool all of the people all of the time. It measures leadership by results and retires those who overreach or falter or fail.

It is true that in the long run despots are measured by results too. But they can postpone the day of judgment, sometimes indefinitely, and in the meantime they can do infinite harm. It is also true that democracy is no guarantee of virtue and intelligence in government, for the voice of the people is not necessarily the voice of God. But democracy, by assuring the right of opposition, offers built-in resistance to the evils inherent in absolutism. As the theologian Reinhold Niebuhr summed it up, "Man's capacity for justice makes democracy possible, but man's inclination to injustice makes democracy necessary."

A second test for leadership is the end for which power is sought. When leaders have as their goal the supremacy of a master race or the promotion of totalitarian revolution or the acquisition and exploitation of colonies or the protection of greed and privilege or the preservation of personal power, it is likely that their leadership will do little to advance the cause of humanity. When their goal is the abolition of slavery, the liberation of women, the enlargement of opportunity for the poor and powerless, the extension of equal rights to racial minorities, the defense of the freedoms of expression and opposition, it is likely that their leadership will increase the sum of human liberty and welfare.

Leaders have done great harm to the world. They have also conferred great benefits. You will find both sorts in this series. Even "good" leaders must be regarded with a certain wariness. Leaders are not demigods; they put on their trousers one leg after another just like ordinary mortals. No leader is infallible, and every leader needs to be reminded of this at regular intervals. Irreverence irritates leaders but is their salvation. Unquestioning submission corrupts leaders and demeans followers. Making a cult of a leader is always a mistake. Fortunately hero worship generates its own antidote. "Every hero," said Emerson, "becomes a bore at last."

The signal benefit the great leaders confer is to embolden the rest of us to live according to our own best selves, to be active, insistent, and resolute in affirming our own sense of things. For great leaders attest to the reality of human freedom against the supposed inevitabilities of history. And they attest to the wisdom and power that may lie within the most unlikely of us, which is why Abraham Lincoln remains the supreme example of great leadership. A great leader, said Emerson, exhibits new possibilities to all humanity. "We feed on genius. . . . Great men exist that there may be greater men."

Great leaders, in short, justify themselves by emancipating and empowering their followers. So humanity struggles to master its destiny, remembering with Alexis de Tocqueville: "It is true that around every man a fatal circle is traced beyond which he cannot pass; but within the wide verge of that circle he is powerful and free; as it is with man, so with communities."

1

The Generalissimo at Bay

He stood at a bedroom window in the small hotel that was serving as his headquarters during his stay at Xian. It was very early on the morning of December 11, 1936, not yet five o'clock, but Chiang Kai-shek was an early riser. As he did each morning, he completed a series of exercises, folded his arms across his chest, stared into the darkness, and tried to meditate, but that morning's contemplation was interrupted by the sound of gunfire from outside the hotel.

It was Chiang's (in Chinese, the family name precedes the given name) fourth morning in Xian, an industrial city on the Wei River, in north-central China's mountainous Shaanxi province. He had arrived aboard his private plane on December 7, having traveled from his capital at Nanjing, some 500 miles to the southeast, to confer with Zhang Xueliang, known as the "Young Marshal." The purpose of the meeting was to enlist Zhang's support for Chiang's planned offensive against the Chinese Communists, led by Mao Zedong, who had established a stronghold in northern China. Their capital

He had grown up in a time of treachery and violence. There were few standards of human decency his warlord contemporaries did not violate; they obeyed no law but power, and Chiang outwitted them at their own game.
—THEODORE WHITE and ANNALEE JACOBY American historians

China's political and military leader, Chiang Kai-shek, and his wife, Mei-ling Soong. Their marriage in December 1927 was a political as much as a love match. Mei-ling wanted power; Chiang regarded her family connections and wealth as indispensable to his future ambitions.

13

The market street in Yanan, Shaanxi province, where the Chinese Communists established their capital in 1936. At Yanan the Communists emphasized redistribution of land and tax relief for the peasantry.

was at Yanan, just 150 miles to the north. Although Chiang contemptuously referred to the Communists as "bandits," his five previous campaigns, involving a successively larger number of forces, had failed to defeat them. Chiang's sixth "bandit-suppression" campaign was intended to completely eliminate the Communists as a political threat.

As the political and military head of the *Guomindang* (Nationalist party), Chiang was the dominant figure in China. His legitimacy as the nation's leader rested in part on the widespread perception that he had inherited the mantle of leadership from Sun Yat-sen, the Western-educated physician who led 10 unsuccessful uprisings against the more than 250-year-old Qing dynasty between 1895 and 1910. Although Sun was in England when the rebellion that finally unseated the Qings broke out in October 1911, and although his subsequent efforts at establishing a Western-style parliamentary democracy in China were failures, he was revered by many Chinese as the "Father of the Revolution." When Chiang emerged as the leader of the Guomindang after Sun's death in March 1925, he assured all that he would carry out Sun's three principles of nationalism, democracy, and socialism. He sought to further solidify his position as the heir apparent to Sun's political legacy by proposing marriage to Sun's widow, the former Ching-ling Soong. When she refused him, he courted her younger sister, Mei-ling, who married him on December 1, 1927. The two girls were the daughters of Charles Soong, who as a young runaway had made his way to the United States, where he was converted to Methodism and educated as a missionary. After his return to China he renounced his vocation (but not his religion), made a fortune publishing and selling Chinese translations of the Bible, and financed Sun's revolutionary efforts. In time their riches and political connections made the Soongs the wealthiest and most influential family in China.

Chiang's greatest claim to legitimacy rested on his military accomplishments. Shortly after the fall of the last of the Qings—the boy emperor Hsuan-t'ung (known in the West as Henry Pu-yi)—in 1912,

Chinese Communist party (CCP) leader Mao Zedong, journalist Earl Leaf, Mao's most trusted general, Zhu De, and an unidentified woman at Yanan. Chiang dismissed the Communists as bandits, but those who visited Yanan found a self-sufficient society governed by a disciplined political and military organization.

China entered into a chaotic period referred to subsequently as the age of the warlords. When the Qing dynasty toppled, it took with it many of China's traditional institutions. Adherents of Western-style democracy proved unable to establish themselves as a governing authority, as did the military leader Yuan Shikai, who attempted to install himself as the first of a new imperial line. With all central authority gone, the warlords—military governors, many of whom had been officers in the imperial army—arose to fill the void.

It was a period when, as the American journalist Theodore White put it, "all those who were accustomed to govern were gone, and the soldiers who took over found with astonishment that they were government." The warlords used their military might to govern entire provinces and regions. They ruled as long as they were able to field sufficient troops to fend off incursions by warlords from neighboring regions or quell mutinies by ambitious underlings. Although some sought to provide the services that formerly had been the responsibility of the central government — highway and waterway maintenance, famine and flood relief — most were concerned only with looting and pillaging the countryside and wringing the last bit of taxes from the helpless populace. Because merchants and the gen-

Two peasants use a hand-powered roller to grind grain. In the 1930s China's peasants were using the same farming methods as had been used for thousands of years. Few peasants owned their own land; most paid a large portion of their yearly crop in rent to absentee landlords.

try were often able to buy protection from the warlords, it was China's peasantry that suffered the most from their privations.

After taking control of the Guomindang, Chiang was determined to carry out Sun's long-cherished plan of a "northern expedition" in order to establish the party as the central government of China. Using revenues available to him through the financial wizardry of T. V. Soong, Ching-ling and Mei-ling's brother, Chiang was able to raise and outfit an army of 100,000 to march on the warlords of the northern provinces. The Nationalist forces left their headquarters at Guangzhou (Canton) in the spring of 1926; by early 1928 most of the warlords had professed their loyalty to Chiang, the Nationalists were collecting taxes in all but a few regions of China, and Chiang was proclaiming himself the leader of a unified nation.

One of the last to capitulate was the Young Marshal's father, Zhang Zuolin, the warlord of Manchuria, which comprises the three northeastern provinces of Liaoning, Jilin, and Heilungkiang. The region was China's leading industrial area and was rich in oil, coal, gold, magnesium, uranium, timber, and other resources. Manchuria's fertile soil and relatively sparse population made it that much more attractive to foreign powers, particularly the Soviet Union and Japan, which both had commercial and strategic interests there and had fought a war over control of the territory in 1904–05. By the time of Chiang's northern expedition, Japan's government was moving closer to a policy of aggressive militarism that envisioned extending Japan's influence in Manchuria and then the rest of China as the first steps toward establishing a Japanese empire in Asia.

The plans of the Japanese militarists had a much better chance of succeeding as long as China was fragmented and weak. Because a united China under a strong central government posed a threat to Japanese interests, the militarists looked with disfavor upon Chiang's northern expedition. When Zhang Zuolin at last professed his loyalty to the Guomindang in the spring of 1928, the Japanese killed him by blowing up his railroad car outside the Manchurian city of Mukden.

Japanese provocation did not end with the elder Zhang's assassination. In September 1931 the Japanese set off an explosion in the Mukden rail yards

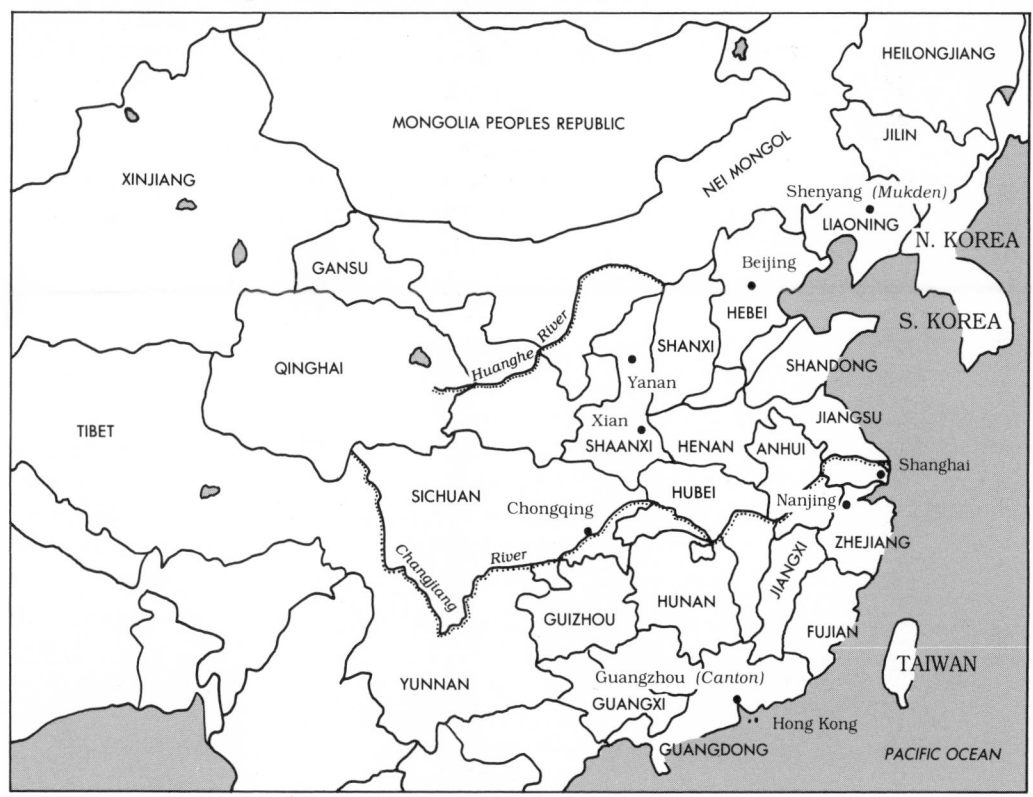

Japanese artillery pounds Chinese positions along the Nen River in Manchuria. Chiang's refusal to combat the Japanese following their September 1931 invasion of Manchuria infuriated patriotic Chinese and led the Manchurian warlord Zhang Xueliang to kidnap him in December 1936.

and used it as a pretext for an attack on that city and ultimately all of Manchuria. The following year the Japanese announced that Manchuria and the province of Jehol constituted the independent state of Manchukuo and installed the displaced Qing emperor Pu-yi as puppet ruler.

Chinese rulers were traditionally measured by their success in quelling internal unrest and repelling foreign aggression. Tired of watching their country carved up by foreign nations and looted by warlords, many patriotic Chinese rejoiced in the Guomindang's early triumphs. These same Chinese were dismayed when Chiang took no action against the Japanese invaders. Chiang believed that his forces were not strong enough to challenge the Japanese, and he was more concerned with exterminating the Communists, who at one time had been allied with the Guomindang but now presented the only real internal challenge to his regime.

Chiang's fifth bandit-suppression campaign had driven the Communists on a 6,000-mile odyssey from Jiangxi province, in southeast China, to Shaanxi. The Guomindang portrayed the Long March, as it is known, as a defeat for the Communists, but it ultimately proved to be a victory. Chiang had aimed at extermination, but the Communists had survived. Although they lost nearly 80 percent of their soldiers and cadres, the Communists gained many new supporters by asserting that they were not retreating but marching north to combat the Japanese.

When the gunfire began that December morning in Xian it did not take Chiang long to assess the situation. Clad only in his nightshirt, he sprinted from his room. Two aides boosted him over a 10-foot wall, but on the other side was an empty moat, and he fell nearly 30 feet, badly injuring his back and spraining an ankle. He still managed to clamber barefoot through the snow up a nearby mountain. Two sweeps by the Young Marshal's soldiers failed to locate him, and it was more than four hours before he was discovered shivering in a small cave. Soldiers took turns carrying him on their backs down the mountainside. He was taken to the town hall, where Zhang Xueliang and Shaanxi warlord Yang Hucheng had their headquarters.

Despite his hesitance in doing so, Chiang was seen as the only man capable of leading a unified resistance to Japan. The nation was stunned by the news that he was being held captive in Xian. The writer Lloyd Eastman observed that with Chiang's kidnapping "a pall of gloom had fallen over most of the nation. Children, it was reported, could not sleep; soldiers wept; and illiterates badgered those who read the newspapers in order to learn the most recent dispatches from Xian."

The Generalissimo, as Chiang was known in the West, was in an unfamiliar position. Mercurial, unpredictable, impulsive, given to violent, towering rages, Chiang was unaccustomed to having his will thwarted. During his rise to power he had often used kidnapping, extortion, torture, and murder against his opponents; he had no reason to believe that his captors would treat him any more benevolently. He would not have been reassured to know that his associates in the Guomindang responded to the news of his abduction by planning to bomb Xian (the scheme had the virtue, in their eyes, of being as likely to kill Chiang as it was to release

He's a vacillating, tricky, undependable old scoundrel who never keeps his word.
—JOSEPH STILWELL, U.S. general, on Chiang

him), nor was his discomfort eased when his old enemy Zhou Enlai, of the Chinese Communist party (CCP), arrived from Yanan a few days after his capture.

Zhang Xueliang's motives were patriotic, but Chiang could not be certain of that. Zhang had succeeded his father as warlord of Manchuria. When the Japanese invaded Manchuria in 1931, he had 400,000 troops under arms, as compared to 85,000 Japanese soldiers, but allowed himself to be restrained by Chiang, who told him that "in order to avoid any enlargement of the incident, it is necessary resolutely to maintain the principle of nonresistance." Shortly after the Japanese completed their takeover, Zhang went to Europe, where he underwent a cure for opium addiction. Until that point something of a playboy, he returned to China two years later single-minded in his determination to pursue a war of resistance against the Japanese. When the Communists arrived in Shaanxi in 1935, cloaked in an aura of invincibility from their feats on the Long March and carrying the banner of anti-Japanese resistance, Zhang was intrigued; when they destroyed two of his divisions in combat that same year he realized that both patriotism and self-interest could be served by making overtures to Mao.

Zhang and Zhou confronted Chiang with a series of demands that effectively added up to one condition for release: Chiang was to lead a "united front"

In Nanjing, his capital city, Chiang (far right), who with the initial success of his northern expedition controlled China to the Huang-he, sought a declaration of loyalty from Zhang Xueliang (far left), who governed Manchuria and much of northern China. At center is Zhang's wife, flanked by Chiang's wife Mei-ling Soong (right) and sister-in-law Ai-ling Soong.

of the Guomindang and CCP against Japan. Specifically, he was to reorganize his government and admit all political parties, who together would pursue "national salvation," that is, resistance to Japan; end the civil war with the communists; carry out a policy of armed resistance to Japan; release all those who had been imprisoned for speaking out against the Japanese and Chiang's government; guarantee the political liberties of the Chinese people, such as freedom of speech and assembly and the right to form political parties; establish Sun Yat-sen's three principles; and assemble a national salvation conference.

Madame Chiang, as the Generalissimo's wife was known, succeeded in halting the planned bombing attack and then hurried to Xian. She was joined there by T. V. Soong. With no real choice, Chiang agreed to lead a united front. He was released on December 25, 1936. Zhang agreed to accompany the Chiangs back to Nanjing as a gesture of his good faith and continuing loyalty; T. V. Soong in turn guaranteed Zhang's safety. Shortly after his arrival in Nanjing, Zhang was seized by Guomindang secret police. His cohort in the abduction, Yang, fled to Europe, but when he returned some years later he, too, was arrested. Yang spent 11 years in a prison camp, and his wife fasted to death in protest of his detention. Zhang spent the rest of his life, more than 40 years, under house arrest, studying the history of China's Ming dynasty, whose rulers were notorious for their brutality and treachery, his days eased somewhat by the heroin generously provided him by his jailers.

The Australian journalist W. H. Donald (right) served as adviser to Zhang (left). An advocate of Chinese unity to repel the Japanese, Donald acted as mediator in helping to secure Chiang's release after his kidnapping.

2
Self-strengthening

Chiang Kai-shek was born on October 31, 1887, in the village of Chikou, 30 miles southwest of the trading center of Ningpo. Chikou is in Zhejiang, one of China's smallest but most densely populated provinces. The boy was the first son of his father's third wife. He had an older half brother and half sister and later two younger sisters and a brother. His given name at birth was Jui-tai, which means "Entire Prosperity," but like many Chinese he acquired new names to signify accomplishments or the beginning of an important new period in his life. The name by which he is known to history, Kai-shek, was acquired in his early days as a revolutionary and is the pronunciation in the Cantonese dialect of the name Chieh-shih, meaning "Between Rocks."

Chiang's father, Su-an, was a salt merchant. Most Chinese ate little or no meat; their staple foods were rice, wheat, and other grains and cereals. This diet provided virtually no salt, which is essential to maintaining human life and health. The position of

> *He was an odd and sickly child, given to fits of ill temper, and became an object of ridicule in the village. . . . He grew up having bouts of weeping and seizures of uncontrollable rage, interspersed by periods of long withdrawal.*
> —STERLING SEAGRAVE
> American author
> on Chiang's childhood

In May 1937 Chiang returned to his home village of Chikou, in Zhejiang province, for the funeral of his brother. During the first 62 years of his life Chiang made periodic retreats to Chikou and the Buddhist monastery at nearby Fenghua.

salt merchant was thus an important and potentially lucrative one. Su-an was the first of his family to engage in trade. At the time of Chiang's birth nearly 80 percent of the Chinese population, which was approaching 500 million, was dependent on agriculture for their living. Previous generations of Chiangs had all been farmers.

As an infant Chiang was sickly and frail, and during several of his illnesses there were doubts about whether he would survive. At the age of three or so his health improved, and he built his strength romping about the hillsides of Chikou. During his adult years he possessed amazing physical strength and stamina. Of all his boyhood games, he most enjoyed playing soldier. His rambunctiousness provided his parents new worries, as he developed a penchant for unlikely accidents, such as getting a pair of chopsticks stuck down his throat or becoming trapped in a large urn used to collect rainwater. None of these escapades did him lasting harm.

When Chiang was four his education was entrusted to a private tutor. He received the traditional Chinese schooling, which consisted of immersion in the philosophical system known as *Confucianism*. K'ung Fu-tzu — the name was rendered in Latin as Confucius — was a minor government official and scholar who lived from 551 to 479 B.C. His teachings and sayings were collected and preserved by his followers. These sayings, along with the interpreta-

Chiang's childhood home in Chikou (right), where he was born on October 31, 1887. His family was initially somewhat prosperous but endured more difficult economic times after the death of his father in 1895.

tions of later scholars, formed the basis of a classical Chinese education. Because learning to read Chinese is so difficult — the language does not have an alphabet, but thousands of characters, or ideograms, that individually or in combination represent ideas, concepts, or things — the traditional method of teaching emphasized rote repetition of passages or characters from the Confucian classics. Students learned to read and write by copying characters over and over. Among younger students, little attention was paid to understanding; teachers assumed that comprehension would come later. By the time he was nine years old, Chiang had been through the four most important of the Confucian classics: *The Great Learning*, *The Middle Way*, and *The Analects*, all attributed to Confucius himself, and *The Sayings*, by the 4th-century B.C. sage Mencius. By the age of 16, Chiang had completed most of the other major works in the Confucian canon.

Although it contains religious elements and rules for religious conduct, Confucianism is not a religion. It is more properly understood as a system of ethical beliefs that seeks to regulate and explain individual and societal conduct, was enshrined by China's imperial dynasties as a state philosophy, and came to form the foundation of Chinese culture. Confucianism seeks to explain how a just and harmonious society can be established and main-

Chinese men during the late Qing (Manchu) period wore long pigtails, called queues, as an emblem of devotion to the imperial family. To cut off one's queue, as Chiang, Sun Yat-sen, and Mao Zedong did, was to proclaim oneself a revolutionary.

The philosophy attributed to the 6th-century B.C. sage Confucius emphasizes a stable, harmonious society achieved through the cultivation of *li*, or right conduct. Confucian thought permeated Chinese culture well into the 20th century.

tained. Positing that in its natural state the universe was complete and in harmony, Confucius and those working in his tradition asserted that society would follow suit when its members fulfilled the responsibilities arising from their position in a hierarchical social system. Fulfillment of these duties constituted "right," or proper, conduct, a concept known in Chinese as *li*.

The basic unit of Confucian society was the family, which bore complete responsibility for all its members. The highest Confucian virtue was therefore filial piety (devotion to familial obligations). There were essentially five social relationships: subject to ruler, wife to husband, son to father, younger brother to elder brother, and friend to friend. Each of the parties within these relationships had certain obligations toward the other. At the top of this society was the emperor, who was understood to rule by virtue of the "mandate of heaven." Virtue flowed outward from individual behavior. To the extent that each person knew his position and acted properly, society would be harmonious and the kingdom would prosper.

Mencius said that "he who delights in Heaven, will affect with his love and protection the whole empire." Not even the emperor was exempt from cultivating li. Indeed, by virtue of his exalted position, the emperor was to be the very embodiment of Confucian virtue, by whose example all others were moved to right conduct. His mandate, or authority, derived from his own virtue. Confucius said simply, "When a prince's personal conduct is correct, his government is effective without the issuing of orders. If his personal conduct is not correct, he may issue orders but they will not be followed." Failure of the emperor to act properly — for example, by imposing ruinous taxation upon the populace — led to such manifestations of a rend in the natural order of the universe as earthquakes, flood, famine, foreign aggression, or internal unrest. The emperor was then said to have lost the mandate, possibly justifying a toppling of the dynasty according to the Confucian precept that "Heaven sees as the people see, Heaven hears as the people hear."

The inculcation of Confucian virtues by China's ruling dynasties promoted a relatively stable society, but it left China unprepared for the increased contact with the industrialized nations of the West that came with the 19th century. The Chinese called their nation *Chung-kuo*, which means the "Central Country" or "Middle Kingdom," and saw it as an oasis of civilization surrounded by barbarians. This conviction of superiority stemmed from the belief that only Chinese society embodied the natural order of the universe through enactment of the Confucian virtues. The Confucian ethos thus offered no inducement to change, for what attraction could change hold for a society that already replicated a harmonious and complete universe? Because it embodied the values of the universe, Confucianism was seen by the Chinese as the zenith of human cultural achievement. Those stray traders who made it to China's shores before the 19th century were hauled to Beijing (Peking), the imperial capital, and told that as barbarians they would have to pay monetary tribute if they wished to conduct business with the empire. Foreign commerce was restricted to the southern port of Guangzhou. The Chinese attitude toward further trade with the West was expressed by the emperor Ch'ien Lung in 1793: "Our Celestial Kingdom possesses all things in prolific abundance and lacks no product within our bor-

A Chinese government official and his family in Yunnan province. Most government officials earned their positions by performing well on the national examinations on the Confucian classics. This administrative class, or gentry, owned most of the land in China.

Yung-yen, the fifth Qing emperor, who ruled from 1796 to 1820. The Qing emperors were Manchurian. Initially regarded by the Chinese as interlopers and usurpers, the early Qings preserved traditional Chinese governmental structures, expanded the nation's territory, and presided over a long period of domestic tranquility.

ders. . . . [We have] no need to import the manufactures of . . . barbarians."

Sailing ships from the West continued to arrive in Guangzhou. The technological advances of the Industrial Revolution in the West — the most important of which was the harnessing of steam and later electricity and gasoline as energy sources — enabled the mass production of goods. Industry and capital slowly replaced agriculture and landownership as the most important sources of wealth. As the most advanced of the newly industrialized European nations, Britain particularly desired increased access to China, both as a market for its consumer goods and as a provider of tea, silk, porcelain, and cotton.

The Qing emperors continued to resist British encroachment. By the early 1800s the British were consuming tea, most of it from China, in large quantities. China still had no interest in British goods, so Britain paid for its tea with the profits made from selling produce from India, its largest and most important colony. Then the British hit upon opium as the perfect product with which to infiltrate the Chinese market. This addictive drug already accounted for 10 percent of Britain's revenues in India, where it was grown. It proved even more profitable in China. In 1800 the British exported 4,500 chests of Indian opium to China; by 1838 that figure had reached 40,000, and the number of addicts in China was estimated at between 2 and 10 million. Although opium was officially prohibited, its addictiveness guaranteed a captive market, and the money to be made on its sale persuaded Chinese customs officials and other middlemen to participate in the trade.

China's attempts to interdict the illicit trade resulted in the Opium War, which lasted from 1839 to 1842. Although opium was the precipitating cause, at stake was the issue of free trade, as the West defined it, as opposed to China's attempts to defend itself from what it viewed as a predatory and inferior culture. The West's technological superiority extended to weaponry and the instruments of modern warfare. China's years of relative isolation had done nothing for the strength of its armed forces. In the words of noted *sinologist* (scholar of Chinese culture) John King Fairbank, "The land troops could neither ride nor shoot and the water troops could not sail or fire a cannon. The officers could only keep the accounts." By 1840 the British had taken control of the entire coast from Guangzhou to Shanghai.

A defeated China was forced to sign the first of what came to be known as the Unequal Treaties in 1842. The first treaty opened up five ports — Shanghai, Guangzhou, Xiamen (Amoy), Foochow, and Ningpo — to foreign trade. In the next 18 years similar treaties were signed with virtually all of the European trading nations and the United States. They had in common extraterritoriality, which provided that a foreign citizen had to be dealt with under the laws and jurisdiction of his own nation for any crime committed on Chinese soil; fixed tariffs, or taxes, on trade; and a most-favored nation clause, which mandated that any right or privilege extended to another trading partner by China would be extended to all. The European nations were also granted or rented land in Chinese cities. The leases called for fixed rents over a long period of time, such as 99 years. These concessions, as they were known, were allowed self-government under the jurisdiction of their consul, or trade representative. They policed themselves, collected their own taxes, and maintained their own roads and facilities.

The victory of the West was devastating to Chinese morale. The technological superiority that enabled the "barbarians" to establish themselves in China seemed to indicate that Western culture might not in fact be inferior. China's technological stagnation was in some ways a product of the Confucian worldview. Because, in Fairbank's words, "China's great tradition was felt to contain all things," there had been no need for China to look outside itself to keep pace with technological innovations.

Chinese society was arranged in a hierarchy of classes. At the top were the scholar-officials, or gentry, followed by farmers, artisans, and merchants. It was possible to move from one class to another.

A Chinese woodcut from 1840 portrays the arrival of a European steamship at Guangzhou. War with Britain over China's attempts to end the opium trade had begun a year earlier, but what was really at stake was China's desire to preserve its traditional mode of existence from Western nations determined to open China to world trade.

Because China has such a large population and only a small percentage of its terrain is suitable for farming, virtually every square foot of arable land is cultivated. Terracing is used to enable planting even on steep hillside surfaces.

One became a member of the gentry by demonstrating proficiency in the Confucian classics on the nationwide examinations that were given periodically. The exams were open to all, but often only the sons of the gentry class could afford the education necessary for success on the tests, so the gentry became a self-perpetuating class. The relative prosperity an official position ensured enabled the gentry over time to become the primary landowning class in China. Confucian thought held that it was the scholar's duty to advise the government. The higher gentry manned the imperial government, while the lesser gentry was responsible for such tasks of local administration as maintaining temples and public roadways, settling disputes, raising militias, and supporting schools.

Confucianism distinguished between mental and physical labor. Mencius wrote that "mental laborers are governors and manual laborers the governed."

The effect was that although the gentry was encouraged to study the classics and contemplate the nature of a just society, it paid little or no attention to such practical measures as agricultural and industrial production. The overwhelming majority of the population worked in agriculture, but less than 20 percent of the land was suitable for cultivating the rice, tea, cotton, wheat, and mulberry trees that were the economy's most important products. A large population was available to work a comparatively small amount of land, which meant that there was little incentive to develop laborsaving methods or machinery. In the 1800s Chinese agriculture was conducted much the same as it had been for centuries.

The first 150 years of Qing rule had been a time of calm and prosperity, as attested to by the doubling of China's population between 1600 and 1800. China's technological stagnation did not allow its economy to keep pace, and by the early days of the 19th century the standard of living was declining as more people sought to earn their living from the same amount of land. The strength of a dynasty was measured by its ability to quell domestic unrest and repel foreign aggression. In the 1850s the Qings faced a giant peasant-based uprising, later known as the Taiping Rebellion. Its leader was Hung Hsiu-ch'uan, who had failed several times at the national examinations.

With the Western traders had come Christian missionaries. Hung had read several of their tracts, and while suffering from a fever had a vision in which it was revealed to him that he was Jesus Christ's brother, the second son of god, and had been entrusted with the mission of saving mankind. He found many adherents among the peasantry, already disenchanted with the Qing dynasty because of their poor standard of living and the heavy taxation extracted from them by corrupt imperial officials. The rebellion began in Jiangxi province in 1850 and by 1853 had moved north of the Changjiang (Yangtze) River and established its capital at Nanjing. At one point the Taiping rebels even threatened Beijing. Taiping society was egalitarian

Opium smokers in Guangzhou in 1919. In the early 19th century the Chinese reluctantly allowed some export trade with Britain but largely refused to purchase British goods. Seeking a more favorable balance of trade, the British exported opium from India to China, and the addictive drug provided them a lucrative market.

but still embraced the Confucian ideal of filial piety. Whereas women in China were expected to play a subordinate role, the Taipings practiced equality of the sexes. Women served as soldiers, officers, and administrators. The traditional practice of footbinding, which prevented the growth of a woman's feet, was prohibited. (For the Chinese, small feet were erotic. Binding the feet of a female child inhibited foot growth, thus enhancing her desirability as she became a young woman. The practice served the added purpose of limiting a woman's mobility, thus both symbolically and practically securing male dominance in Chinese society.) The Taipings also outlawed promiscuity, slavery, prostitution, gambling, adultery, witchcraft, alcohol, tobacco, and opium.

At the same time, the Qings faced new challenges from the West. After the Opium War the Qings sought to preserve the notion of Chinese superiority by confining the Westerners to the treaty ports and otherwise ignoring their presence. Westerners at court in Beijing were forced to acknowledge their inferiority by kowtowing and paying token monetary tribute to the emperor. In 1858 British and French forces marched on Beijing and burned the emperor's summer palace to the ground. The imperial government had little choice but to sign a new treaty that opened up 11 more treaty ports to the signatories (Britain, France, Russia, and the United States), granted them trading rights in the interior, and promised that their diplomats would be treated as equals.

Internal unrest was not good for business, so British troops under Charles George "Chinese" Gordon now joined with imperial forces to crush the Taiping Rebellion, which had already been weakened by internal dissension and the death of several of its most prominent leaders. With the capture of Nanjing and the suicide of Hung in 1864, the rebellion came to an end. More than 20 million people had been killed during the course of its 14 years.

Foreign encroachment continued during the next 30 years. Britain had concessions at Shanghai, Guangzhou, Xiamen, Chinkiang, Kiukiang, Han-

kow, Tianjin (Tientsin), and Newchang; France at Guangzhou, Shanghai, Hankow, and Tianjin. Extraterritoriality was extended to Denmark, the Netherlands, Spain, Belgium, Italy, Austria-Hungary, and Prussia. Scattered rebellions plagued the imperial administration. China fought wars over Indochina (present-day Vietnam, Cambodia, Laos, and Thailand) with France in 1885, and over Korea with Japan in 1895, and lost both.

During the same time disgruntled scholars and officials were coming to believe that China must emulate the West if it was to save itself. The scholar Wei Yuan counseled that China must "learn the superior technology of the barbarians in order to control them." The movement to learn Western ways so as to increase the might of the nation was known as self-strengthening. Because the Chinese had been most impressed by the weaponry of the Europeans and the Americans, attention was given

The traditional Chinese worldview held their nation to be an oasis of civilization surrounded by barbarians. The Great Wall was begun in the 3rd century B.C. to repel nomadic invaders from the north. It runs 1,500 miles from near the Strait of Pohai to Gansu province.

This woodcut from the 1850s illustrates the antiforeign sentiment prevalent in China during the period, a time when Western nations were using military might to extend their privileges. The print shows members of the gentry burning Western books and directing the beating of foreigners.

first to military matters. Arsenals and shipyards were built, but self-strengthening was unaccompanied by serious efforts at internal reform and did not achieve the success in China that it did in Japan. Two hundred and fifty years of self-imposed isolation had ended for Japan in 1854 with the arrival of American ships, but by the 20th century the Japanese had adopted Western technology and methods, industrialized, overhauled their governmental structure, and stood ready to challenge the West for empire. Five years later Japan defeated Russia in a war fought partially over conflicting interests in Manchuria.

China moved into the 20th century with a good deal less confidence. The peasantry was reeling under the burden of excessive taxation. As the population increased, land was harder to come by, and much of it was ruined during the many uprisings that bedeviled the Qings. In 1898 the Huanghe (Yellow) River flooded, and the reserves in the imperial granaries were insufficient to ward off famine. The north was plagued by drought. During the "One Hundred Days" of 1898 Emperor Kuang-hsu attempted to implement wide-ranging measures aimed at ending corruption of government officials, establishing state-sponsored public education, abolishing the examination system, and reorganizing government institutions, but his plans were thwarted by his aunt and adoptive mother, the murderous and treacherous Empress Dowager Ci Xi, who wielded the true imperial power. Described by the historian C. P. Fitzgerald as "the forceful woman of few scruples who dominate[d] a decadent court,"

Ci Xi used her control of court officials and the armed forces to put a stop to the reform movement. Kuang-hsu wound up a virtual prisoner in the imperial palace, known as the Forbidden City, and six of the most prominent reform advocates were executed.

At the same time a new peasant movement was gaining strength. The Society of Righteous and Harmonious Fists, or Boxers, intended to purge China of Western influence. The Boxers' particular target was Christian missionaries, and in its earliest incarnation the society also meant to overthrow the decadent Qing dynasty. As the movement became more powerful, the empress dowager was shrewd enough to see that perhaps the Boxers could succeed where the government had failed and drive the Westerners from China. She cultivated the group, whose motto became "uphold the Qing, exterminate the foreigner." The Boxers burned Christian churches and attacked missionaries and Chinese Christians throughout northern China. On June 13, 1900, 140,000 Boxers entered Beijing and laid siege to the 11 foreign legations there. That same week the Boxers invaded Tianjin, the imperial government declared war on the West, and imperial troops fired on British forces. The siege continued until August 14, when the legations were liberated by allied forces from Russia, the United States, Japan, and Britain. A German army conducted mopup operations in the north for months afterward. The Boxer Protocol, which the 11 Western nations forced China to sign, required the execution of 10 Chinese high officials, formal apologies, the sus-

At the end of the 19th century Chinese resentment against the West culminated in the Boxer Rebellion. When the western legations and settlements in Beijing and other cities were attacked, an international army was dispatched to quell the uprising. Pictured is an American artillery regiment in action.

pension of exams, expansion of the legation quarter, destruction of Chinese forts, and the payment of massive reparations.

Chiang became aware at a young age that the Qing dynasty was corrupt and tottering. He wrote later about his youth that he "remembered that the Manchu [Qing] regime was in its most corrupt state. The degenerated gentry and corrupt officials had made it a habit to abuse and maltreat the people. My family, solitary and without influence, became at once the target of such insults and maltreatments. From time to time usurious taxes and unjust public service were forced upon us."

Chiang's father died in 1895, and the family found itself in straitened economic circumstances. Chiang wrote that "the miserable condition of my family at that time is beyond description." He became very close to his mother. She was by many accounts a domineering woman who did not hesitate to beat him, but Chiang said that it was through her "kindness and perseverance that the family was saved from utter ruin." At one point a resident of Chikou vanished without paying his rice tax. Chiang was hauled into court and told he would be jailed if he did not provide the missing money. He was humiliated and enraged by this arbitrary exercise of power and referred to the incident as "the first spark that kindled my revolutionary fire."

At the age of 14 Chiang entered into an arranged marriage with Mao Fu-mei, who was 3 years older than he. The marriage was an unhappy one. As was customary, Fu-mei moved into the Chiang family home, where she was expected to defer not only to her husband but to her mother-in-law. Chiang's inability to control his temper showed itself, and he often beat his new bride.

The family's economic situation was not so dire that Chiang was forced to give up his schooling. In 1904 he began work with a new tutor, Ku Ching-lien, at the Pavilion of Literature in nearby Fenghua. The curriculum included more classics, but Chiang was also introduced to Sun Tzu's *The Art of War.* From Sun he learned that "the supreme art of war is to subdue the enemy without fighting" and that "all warfare is based on deception." He studied the works of Tseng Kuo-fan, the Chinese general who joined with the British to subdue the Taiping Rebellion, and Tseng was to remain a lifelong hero. Ku taught him the works of the Confucian philosopher Chu Hsi, who emphasized self-discipline and self-denial. His new instructor was also among the first to speak to the young man of the revolutionary exploits of Dr. Sun Yat-sen. It was at this point that Chiang began his daily habit of meditation.

It was nearing time for him to settle on a career. Like many young Chinese of the day Chiang had vague patriotic notions. He believed that China had to expel the Westerners and that to do so the nation had to build its military strength. He thought he could best serve his country as a soldier, and the best place to learn the art of war was in Japan, whose military might China envied.

Chiang left the Pavilion of Literature, spent three months at the Dragon River Middle School, and then readied himself to go to Japan. Before he left he cut off his *queue*, the long pigtail Chinese men wore as a badge of devotion to the imperial dynasty. The illegal act proclaimed the young man a revolutionary. He left China in the spring of 1905.

Imprisoned Boxers after the failure of the rebellion. The empress dowager had hoped to use the Boxers to expel the foreigners, but their failure illustrated anew the impotence of the Qing dynasty. The victorious Western nations forced China to pay huge reparations and grant them further rights and privileges.

3
At School in the Revolution

Young revolutionaries were no more welcome in Japan than they were in China. Like China, Japan was a monarchy, headed by an imperial dynasty. Although Japan adopted such features of Western democracy as a constitution and representative legislative assembly, its modernization left many traditional Japanese institutions intact. The emphasis was on strengthening existing structures rather than on revolutionary change, and reform had been rapid but essentially conservative. Voting and other democratic rights were limited to an extremely small percentage of the population, and political power was wielded by the emperor and his advisers. Because internal unrest in China enabled Japan to further its interests there, Japan sometimes provided refuge to exiled Chinese revolutionaries — such as Sun Yat-sen — but it did not wish revolutionary ideals to take hold among its own populace.

The Japanese military establishment was a particular bastion of conservatism. Chiang was thus unable to gain admission to any of the military academies. He knocked about Tokyo for several months. The most important contact he made at this time

When I was a young man, I made up my mind to become a soldier. I have always believed that to be in the army is the highest experience of human existence as well as the highest form of revolutionary activity.
—CHIANG KAI-SHEK

With the death of the empress dowager and her nephew and adoptive son, the Emperor Kuang-hsu, in November 1908, the three-year-old Hsuan-t'ung (known also as Pu-yi, shown here on his father's lap) became emperor. His father, Prince Ch'un, acted as regent. Three years later the Qing dynasty would be overthrown by republican and military forces.

Sun Yat-sen was trained as a physician but devoted his life to overthrowing the Qings and establishing a modern national government for China. Although Sun is revered by both Communist and Nationalist Chinese as the father of the revolution, his own attempts at rebellion failed, and he was abroad when the successful 1911 uprising began.

was Ch'en Ch'i-mei, a loyal supporter of Sun. By the winter of 1905 he was back in China, laying new plans for military school. The following year he was one of 60 students from Zhejiang (out of more than 1,000) to pass the entrance exam for the Japanese-run Paoting Military Academy, but even then his admission was not assured. His short hair continued to identify him as a revolutionary, and he was of Han Chinese lineage, not Manchu like the Qings and their most powerful advisers and military men. Nevertheless, he was admitted. His classmates found him conceited and aloof, and his patriotism brought him into conflict with his Japanese instructors, but after a year's study he was one of only a few students selected to go to Japan for further instruction.

In the spring of 1907 he enrolled in Tokyo's *Shinbo Gakyo* (Preparatory Military Academy). While there he renewed his friendship with Ch'en Ch'i-mei. The most important event of his two-year stint at the academy was his introduction to Sun Yat-sen, by Ch'en, in early 1908.

Sun was nearly 21 years older than Chiang. His parents were peasants from near Guangzhou, in Guangdong province. His uncle had fought with the Taipings, and Sun's boyhood idol was Hung Hsiu-ch'uan. At the age of 13 he was sent to Hawaii to be raised in the care of an older brother. He returned three years later and was educated as a physician in Hong Kong, where he also became a Christian.

When Chiang met him, Sun had long since traded medicine for revolution. He had already failed in several attempts at rebellion. At this point Sun was more concerned with overthrowing the Qings than with what form China's future government should take. Sun was never a systematic or sophisticated political thinker. His theories were later collected and published in *San Min Chu I* (*The Three Principles of the People*), a transcription of a series of lectures. The first of the three principles was nationalism, which Sun defined as anti-Qing, anti-foreign, and prorepublican. The second principle, democracy, was to take the form of elected councils for his five branches of government — the legislative,

judicial, executive, civil service, and censorial. The people would have the right to vote, remove officials, and initiate proposals, but full democracy would come into existence only as the final step in Sun's three-stage program. Democracy would be preceded by three years of military government and six of "tutelage," which meant essentially rule by Sun's political party, the *Zhongguo Tong Meng Hui* (translated as the Chinese United League or the Alliance Society, which was succeeded in 1912 by the Guomindang). The final principle Sun called socialism. He said later that socialism meant communism, but as he originally envisioned it socialism meant a tax

The years 1907 to 1911 were marked by frequent armed rebellions against the Qings. The revolutionary fireworks began with an uprising of discontented soldiers in Guangdong province in May 1907 that was easily suppressed by imperial troops.

on increases in land value and did not imply a redistribution of land or property.

Chiang joined the Tong Meng Hui and volunteered his services to Sun, who told him to remain in school. One reason for the failure of Sun's rebellions was that he was forced to make use of mercenaries, gangsters, criminals, and peasants and workers as his fighting force. The movement lacked accomplished military men; a Japanese-trained officer could prove to be of inestimable value. Shortly after Chiang joined the Tong Meng Hui the Japanese government deported Sun, and he went to Hong Kong, from where he directed several more unsuccessful uprisings.

That same year Chiang's wife, who had remained with his mother in Chikou, gave birth to their first son, Ching-kuo, but the marriage continued to be an unhappy one. Although Chiang had earned a reputation at Shinbo Gakyo as an ascetic for his Spartan eating habits and self-discipline—he subsisted on two bowls of rice a day and a small portion of fish—he was beginning to familiarize himself with the numerous brothels of Shanghai on his visits home.

Chiang graduated from Shinbo Gakyo in November 1909. He wished to continue his training at the Military University but was required to serve a term in the Japanese army first. He was assigned to the 19th Field Artillery Regiment at Takada but made no impression on his superior officers during his brief tour of duty.

In China the empress dowager approved reform programs, hoping thereby to slow the development of revolutionary and republican movements. The traditional examination system was maintained, but the government established a system of schools at the provincial and local levels. Emulating the Japanese educational system, provincial officials liberalized the curriculum. Confucian classics were still taught, but so were such Western writers as the novelists Charles Dickens, Honoré de Balzac, and Victor Hugo, the philosopher John Stuart Mill, the economist Adam Smith, and the political theorist Charles Montesquieu. Similar reforms took place in the military. Yuan Shikai, who had been a Chinese military governor in Korea and the man the empress dowager turned to for support during the One Hundred Days crisis, remodeled much of the army along German lines.

The empress dowager died on November 15, 1908. Her death was preceded by a day by that of Emperor Kuang-hsu, and it was rumored that she had had him poisoned. Three-year-old Pu-yi, the empress dowager's grandnephew, became the new emperor, with his father, Prince Ch'un, as regent.

For the majority of China's young, educated people, the Qing dynasty's tentative steps toward reform were inadequate. Most wanted either the abolition of the dynasty or the establishment of a constitutional monarchy and looked to Japan, which in the words of China scholars Franz Schurmann and Orville Schell "provided China with a close and culturally homogenous sanctuary in which the Chinese Revolution could incubate," as a model. Fairbank said that "Republican China went to school in Tokyo." At the same time, a new class of military officers, trained by Japanese or Western military instructors, was dissatisfied with the situation in China, particularly its domination by foreign nations.

On October 9, 1911, troops rebelled in the city of Wuchang, the provincial capital of Hubei. The terrified governor fled, and the city was soon in the hands of the rebels. Other uprisings followed, most led by disgruntled military units, and by December the southern, central, and northwest provinces were in various stages of revolt. Chiang had returned from Japan and played a minor part in the fighting by leading a small force that set fire to the governor's mansion at Hangchow, the capital of Zhejiang. Sun was in London, England, when the rebellions began, but he hurried home and was inaugurated on January 1, 1912, as the provisional president of the republican government established at Nanjing.

The soldiers were soon joined by students and intellectuals. The beleaguered imperial officials turned to Yuan Shikai. Many of the provincial mil-

The empress dowager, Ci Xi, was the real ruler of China from 1875 to 1908, during the reign of her nephew, Kuang-hsu. A steadfast opponent of innovation, the empress dowager used the armed forces to thwart the reforms advocated by Kuang-hsu during the 100 Days of 1898.

itary officers had served under Yuan, and the government believed he was the one man who might be able to command the loyalty of the army. The republicans were thinking the same way. Hoping to avoid civil war and possible foreign intervention, Sun offered to resign the presidency in favor of Yuan if he would support the republic.

Yuan carried a grudge against the regent, Prince Ch'un, who had relieved him of his posts upon the death of the empress dowager. Pu-yi's advisers hoped that Yuan would defend the government, but instead he offered the republicans the emperor's resignation in exchange for the presidency. The six-year-old emperor had no choice but to abdicate. He was allowed to retain his title, court, and some of his revenues and remain in residence in the Forbidden City.

The essence of the revolutionary movement had been its insistence on replacing the Qings, but the dynasty's collapse revealed that its successors were unprepared to govern. In the words of Schurmann and Schell, "Before the Revolution the Manchus [Qings] were a convenient scapegoat for all of China's problems, but their collapse meant that men like Sun Yat-sen had to look beyond the anti-Manchu whipping post and confront a plethora of staggeringly complex problems, most of which, it soon became obvious to anyone who cared to look, China was ill-equipped to deal with." The revolutionaries had also proclaimed the importance of ending China's economic dependence, but Yuan's new govern-

The rebellion that overthrew the Qing dynasty began in the city of Wuchang in October 1911. Republicans and dissatisfied army officers combined to force the abdication of Pu-yi in February 1912. Pictured is the destruction in the city of Hankow.

ment was insufficiently strong to collect taxes, which made it necessary for him to turn to the Western nations for revenue. He borrowed money from a consortium of British, French, German, Russian, Japanese, and U.S. banks, giving control of the government's salt tax as collateral.

A legislative body, the National Assembly, was elected by an extremely limited popular vote and was convened at Nanjing, but its members had no experience at lawmaking and spent much of their time voting themselves pay raises. In August 1912 the Guomindang was formed and soon became the most important party in the assembly. Yuan did not understand democratic processes. He intended to gather all political power to himself, regarded political parties as a threat, and had several prominent Guomindang leaders assassinated, the most important of them Song Jiaoren. In November 1913 Yuan outlawed the Guomindang. A year later Yuan dissolved the assembly, and in 1916 he announced that he planned to have himself crowned emperor.

Chiang returned to school in Japan at about the time the Guomindang was formed. At the Military University he edited the newspaper the *Voice of the Army* from 1912 to 1913. His first editorials named Japan and Russia as China's most likely enemies and argued that the practice of giving China's provincial governors complete military and civil authority for their regions would ultimately make China impossible to govern.

During the summer and at other school breaks Chiang returned to China. He sometimes stopped briefly at home, but most of his free time was spent in Shanghai, usually in the company of Ch'en Ch'i-mei. Shanghai was China's financial and trading center and was also known for its riotous nightlife and treacherous underworld. One out of every 12 houses was a brothel, and 1 out of every 130 persons was a prostitute. Chiang threw off his customary self-discipline and, in the words of an acquaintance, "abandoned himself to a life of intense dissipation." He took a prostitute, Yao Yi-ching, as his mistress. She sometimes accompanied him to Tokyo and was most likely the mother of his second son, Wei-kuo.

During the 1911 revolution the republicans and those loyal to the Qings vied for the support of Yuan Shikai, the former military governor of the Chinese province of Korea and the man to whom the empress dowager had turned during the 100 Days crisis. Yuan persuaded Pu-yi to abdicate and was elected president, but he soon began eliminating possible political opponents and gathering power to himself.

Secret societies were a prominent part of Chinese life. Many were begun as self-help and revolutionary organizations that united Chinese from the same region or family background, but in time some became criminal groups. One of the most notorious of these was Shanghai's Green Gang, which controlled the city's prostitution and opium rackets and was closely tied to the business community. Its members were armed, and the organization had little fear of the police. Ch'en was a member of the Green Gang and apparently introduced Chiang to the organization's head, Tu Yueh-sheng. Polish journalist Ilona Ralf Sues described Tu as the "most powerful man in China . . . a combination of Al Capone and Rockefeller." According to an American journalist, Sterling Seagrave, Chiang proved his mettle to his underworld friends by shooting T'ao Ch'eng-chang, a revolutionary whom Ch'en regarded as a rival. Seagrave reports that Chiang committed other murders and bank robberies with Ch'en and that police records for the British concession in Shanghai reveal that he was indicted for murder, extortion, and armed robbery.

The southern provinces were the center of republican sentiment in China, and in the summer of 1913 they rose against Yuan. Chiang had been preparing to go to Germany to continue his education, but when fighting broke out he served as chief of staff to Ch'en, who was acting as Guomindang commander at Shanghai. Yuan had little trouble quelling the rebellion, and Sun and other Guomindang leaders were forced into exile. Both Sun and Chiang fled to Japan, where Chiang spent the next months studying military history and Chinese philosophy. He returned periodically to China to carry out duties for the Guomindang. In the spring of 1914 he was sent to foment a revolt in Shanghai, but his efforts failed due to faulty intelligence. That June he was sent to report on the situation in Manchuria but concluded that there was little likelihood of rebellion there. The following year he again led a failed uprising at Shanghai.

In the meantime Europe had plunged into World War I. The immediate cause was the assassination of the heir to the throne of Austria-Hungary, Archduke Franz Ferdinand, but at stake were the imperial ambitions of the European powers. Japan sided with the Allies (Britain, France, and Russia) against the Central Powers (Germany, Austria-Hungary, and the Ottoman Empire) and marched into the Chinese city of Tsingtao, which the Germans were leasing. From there Japanese troops fanned out across the entire Shandong (Shantung) Peninsula. Japan then pressed upon Yuan's government the Twenty-one Demands, which among other things insisted that China buy half its war supplies from Japan, come to Japan for any loans it might wish to negotiate, allow a Japanese police force to administer certain Chinese cities, employ Japanese military, economic, and political advisers, transfer Germany's leaseholds on the Shandong Peninsula to Japan, and extend Japan's rights in Manchuria. The demands were seen as an intolerable affront to China's sovereignty and almost immediately brought to an end the goodwill patriotic Chinese had developed toward Japan. Strikes, anti-Japanese rallies, and boycotts of Japanese goods followed.

Yuan proceeded with plans for his coronation, but the Japanese actions had demonstrated that he was no more able to defend China from the barbarians than the Qings had been. Recognizing Yuan's weakness, army rebels in Yunnan province rose against him in December 1915. The revolt was followed by others, and in March 1916 Yuan dropped his plans. Before he died three months later, however, he continued his campaign against the Guomindang and had Ch'en assassinated.

Yuan's death left China with no central government. Sun was eager for the Guomindang to fill that role, but China's provincial military governors, or warlords, also recognized in Yuan's death an opportunity to gain power. Virtually all of the warlords had been officers in the imperial army; several had served under Yuan. Most still commanded the loyalty of trained and experienced troops, which put Sun at a disadvantage. For the next 10 years the warlords battled for control of China, with whom-

Each warlord had his own army, each army its district. The great warlords governed entire provinces; their generals governed parts of provinces; their captains governed counties, cities, towns. Three hundred men could keep a county in subjection, levy taxes on it, rape its women, carry off its sons, batten on its crops.
—THEODORE WHITE
American historian, on
China under the warlords

ever was in temporary control of Beijing recognized by the foreign powers as China's national government. The warlords soon recognized, as the American writers Theodore White and Annalee Jacoby put it, that "the state rest[ed] on force." C. P. Fitzgerald described their regimes: "They supported or betrayed the government for money; they warred upon each other to secure richer revenues, they organized the opium trade, sold the official ports, taxed the people for years in advance, squeezed the merchants, and finally, immensely rich, allowed, for a last payment, their troops to be defeated, and retired to the society and ease of the foreign concessions in Shanghai or the British colony of Hong Kong." Fairbank explained how the requisite characteristics of the warlord translated into the rapacious behavior that did so much damage to China: "A warlord had to have a strong personality, subordinate officers and troops. His problem was to feed and supply them all. For this he needed support from the revenues of a great city, a province, a trade route or railway, or from other militarists or a foreign power. The geography of a region might give him a strategic advantage, but its land and people could provide only food and manpower to be requisitioned, not a true territorial base in the modern guerrilla sense, with support among the peasantry. The typical warlord army had no roots among the local people but was a scourge upon them, exacting taxes, living off the villages, feared and despised. An army moving to a new province might therefore better itself, at least temporarily. It was both parasitic and peripatetic."

Chiang's exact whereabouts during the early days of this tumultuous period are uncertain. It is likely that he spent much of his time in Shanghai, where he supported himself as a jobber, or broker in speculative and possibly fraudulent stock issues. It is said that he made a small fortune, more than a million dollars, but dissipated it in licentious living. Sun had other matters on his mind. In 1915 he had married Ching-ling Soong, thereby cementing his alliance with the Soongs, who had provided much of the Guomindang's financing. The family now included the extremely wealthy H. H. Kung, husband of the eldest Soong daughter, Ai-ling. Under the protection of a friendly southern warlord, Sun proclaimed himself head of a nominally republican government at Guangzhou in September 1917, but the alliance was an uneasy one. It soon became obvious to him that what was needed was the military strength to subdue the fractious warlords, and in May 1918 he resigned and retired to Shanghai to plan his next move.

With the end of World War I in November 1918 China eagerly awaited the peace conference to follow. When the United States entered the war in early 1917 on the side of the Allies, President Woodrow Wilson announced that the war was being fought to "make the world safe for democracy." In January 1918 he outlined his war aims in the famous Fourteen Points. Most important among them, from the Chinese perspective, was the abolition of secret diplomacy and the just settlement of colonial claims. Patriotic Chinese, particularly students, took Wilson's message to heart, believing it to be a promise that China would now be allowed to control its own destiny, free of foreign intervention. They had every expectation that the victorious Allies would begin by ordering Japan to relinquish its hold on the Shandong Peninsula.

When the Paris Peace Conference convened, however, it was soon apparent that the only colonial claims to be adjusted were those of the defeated nations. The former colonies of the Central Powers

At the Paris Peace Conference following World War I, the desire of U.S. president Woodrow Wilson (seated, far right) to address colonial issues was thwarted by the leaders of the other major victors, Georges Clemenceau of France (seated, second from right), David Lloyd George of Great Britain (seated, second from left) and to a lesser extent Vittorio Orlando of Italy (seated, far left).

Students in Beijing demonstrate against Japan in April 1920. The anti-Japan movement had begun the previous May with the revelation that the delegates at the Paris Peace Conference would not compel Japan to return control of the Shandong Peninsula to China.

in Africa and the Middle East were redistributed among the victors, who retained virtually all their former territories. France and Britain were particularly vehement in insisting that there be no disruption of the status quo. Wilson feared losing support for what he regarded as his most important idea, the formation of an international peacekeeping organization called the League of Nations, and dared not press the issue. Japan was allowed to retain Shandong.

The news was greeted in China as a betrayal. Outrage was aggravated by the revelation that in the war's final days the government at Beijing had "gladly agreed" to Japan's request that it be allowed to keep Shandong. On May 4, 1919, a giant demonstration took place in Beijing to protest the actions of the peace conference. The participants were mostly students from the university there. The rally began peacefully, but by the end of the day the homes of several government officials deemed responsible for the secret agreement with Japan were burned and looted. The police arrested numerous protesters. In the ensuing weeks there were widespread strikes in sympathy with the arrested students and boycotts of Japanese goods.

The outburst of nationalist feeling and activity thus provoked became known as the May 4th Movement. China's weakness — helplessness even — had again been exposed for the world to see. University students in China had traditionally been active politically, but with the breakdown of central authority the usual channels of involvement — examinations and service as government officials — no longer existed. Within the new nationalist movement an emphasis was placed on "New Culture" and "New Youth." Anything traditional was seen to have been thoroughly discredited. The May 4th Movement was accompanied by an explosion of publishing. Newspapers, magazines, and pamphlets abounded, most debating what direction China should move in. The effort to promote literature written in the spoken Chinese vernacular, rather than the classical written language, was seen by the Western-educated professor Hu Shih as an act of rebellion, "a movement of conscious protest against many of the ideas and institutions in the traditional culture, and of conscious emancipation of the individual man and woman from the bondage of the forces of tradition."

The importance of change in Chinese history and the contributions of the lower classes, rather than the gentry, was emphasized. Hu Shih wrote that he "found the true history of Chinese literature to consist in a series of revolutions, the initiative always coming from the untutored but unfettered people." The journalist and dean of letters at the University of Beijing, Ch'en Tu-hsiu, a leader of the New Youth and New Culture movements, wrote that it was the new generation's obligation "to fight Confucianism, the old tradition of virtue and rituals, the old ethics and the old politics . . . the old learning and the old literature." Although immersion in Western ideas was still seen as essential — Hu Shih wrote that contact with the West "brings new standards of value with which the native culture is re-examined and re-evaluated, and conscious reformation and regeneration are the natural outcome of such transvaluation and values" — it would soon become clear that democracy was one of the institutions left discredited.

Chiang was far from Beijing. He had been asked by Sun to take command of troops in Guangzhou, but he disliked the post. He discovered that his soldiers were only nominally loyal to the Guomindang. All were from Guangzhou or the province of Guangdong and resented taking orders from a native of Zhejiang. Chiang's exacting discipline earned him their enmity, and he was frustrated by his inability to make Sun understand that the loyalty of these forces was dubious at best and that he stood in imminent danger of betrayal. He solved his problem by resigning and returning to Shanghai.

When the news of the Paris Peace Conference reached us we were greatly shocked. We at once awoke to the fact that foreign nations were still selfish and militaristic and that they were all great liars.
—anonymous graduate of Beijing University on the origins of the May 4th Movement

4

A Disease of the Heart

Sun relied increasingly on Chiang but was worried by his irascibility. He managed to persuade Chiang to return to Guangzhou in September 1920. In a letter written shortly afterward, Sun told Chiang, "You have a fiery temper and your hatred of mediocrity is excessive. And it so often leads to quarreling and difficulty in cooperating. As you are shouldering the great and terrible responsibility of our party, you should sacrifice your ideals a little and try to compromise." In a later letter Sun wrote: "You . . . are extremely self-willed to an almost incorrigible extent. Whenever you are disappointed at some trifle, you let your anger go unchecked." The volatility that Sun referred to extended into Chiang's personal life. Having fallen in love with another Shanghai prostitute, Ch'en Chieh-ju, he divorced his wife. He wrote of her: "For the past ten years, I have not been able to bear the sound of hearing her footsteps or seeing her shadow. To this day there has been no home worthy of the name. My decision to divorce her is the result of ten years' painful experience."

In April 1921 a hastily convened parliament elected Sun provisional president of China. He

A slim man, rigid in posture whether erect or seated, always immaculate . . . he behaved with ice-stiff self-discipline—except for the moments when he flew into a tantrum, yelled, threw teacups or plates about, tore up papers and raged out of control.
—THEODORE WHITE
American historian
on Chiang

Generalissimo Chiang Kai-shek in 1930. Although by this time Chiang had established himself as the supreme military and political leader of China, he had been unable to eliminate his most dangerous political rivals, the Chinese Communists.

again made his headquarters in Guangzhou, where it was his turn to receive some advice from Chiang. Sun, Chiang believed, was somewhat naive, too concerned with the niceties of form when he should be paying attention to the realities of power. Stop worrying about parliamentary affairs, such as whether you have been rightfully declared the president of China, Chiang told him, and concentrate on military matters. Chiang was convinced that the Guomindang's immediate goal should be to unify the south. When that was accomplished, the Guomindang could march on Beijing and establish a central government. "The unification of China is not a difficult task," he told Sun.

However, Sun was still dependent on the sufferance of the southern warlords. In June 1922 he and his supporters were driven from Guangzhou by forces loyal to Chen Jiongming, the so-called Hakka General. (The Hakkas were northern Chinese who had migrated to the south centuries earlier but still constituted a distinct cultural group.) Sun was almost killed during the bombardment of his home and finally found refuge on a gunboat anchored at Huangpu (Whampoa), an island near Guangzhou. Chiang had been in Shanghai when the fighting began but hurried to Huangpu to be with Sun. They spent 56 days hiding aboard the gunboat — Chiang passed some of the time reading Sherlock Holmes stories — before retreating to Shanghai in early August.

An international conference was held in Washington, D.C., in late 1921 and early 1922. Because the Western nations were now concerned with restraining Japan, whose growing strength posed a threat to their interests in Asia, they persuaded Japan to return Shandong to China. This action was not sufficient to undo the disillusionment brought on by the betrayal at Paris, however, particularly as the Washington conference left the Unequal Treaties intact.

The notion of establishing a democratic or republican form of government in China was one casualty of this disillusionment. To many educated Chinese, democracy was implicated in the chaos into which China had tumbled after the fall of the Qings. Fitzgerald wrote that the Western nations were unable to see "that in this sad period of disorder democracy and with it all that the West hoped to see flourish in China had been discredited and cast aside. . . . In the name of Parliament they had seen gross and shameless corruption; in the name of democracy they had seen nothing but weak and bad government, military usurpation, violation of law, every kind of oppression and national decline." It was the Western democracies that controlled China's coal mines and dominated trade in the south from Hong Kong; the Western nations that maintained concessions in Shanghai and Tianjin and legations in Beijing. The Western democracies maintained the Unequal Treaties, ran the maritime customs, post office, and salt monopoly and collected and kept their revenues. It was the Western democracies whose steamships and gunboats sailed China's rivers and waterways.

In the summer of 1921, 12 men met in Shanghai and founded the Chinese Communist party (CCP). Among them were the leader of the New Youth and New Culture movement, Ch'en Tu-hsiu; the librarian at the University of Beijing, Li Ta-chao; and a young, educated peasant from Hunan province, Mao Zedong. The delegates represented 57 different

Chiang's future nemesis Mao Zedong (far right) poses with his father, Jenshen (second from left), brother Zetan (far left), and an unidentified man in November 1919. The young peasant from Hunan was about to begin his study of socialism. In two years he would be one of the founding members of the Chinese Communist party (CCP).

groups devoted to studying communist theory and determining how to apply it to China.

The most important exponent of communist thought was Karl Marx, the 19th-century German philosopher and economic historian. With his collaborator, Friedrich Engels, Marx proposed that the driving force of human history was class struggle. The capitalist, industrial nations of the West had reached the stage in their development where capital and ownership of the means of production were concentrated in the hands of a class Marx called the *bourgeoisie*, who prospered by extracting profit from the labor of the working class, called the *proletariat*.

Marx believed that man's consciousness developed in response to his economic needs and the material conditions under which he lived. Interested primarily in increasing profits, the bourgeoisie paid its workers the lowest possible wage that would keep them alive and working, but this left the capitalist system prone to depressions and other disturbances, as the relatively impoverished proletariat, who outnumbered the bourgeoisie, was rendered unable to consume at a rate sufficient to keep the economy healthy. Eventually the proletariat would be awakened to its circumstances and would rise up, smash the state — which was itself a reflection of the capitalist economy — and establish a new society. For Marx, this was the inevitable next step in an ongoing historical process, as unavoidable as the earlier destruction of the monarchies that had presided over feudal economies by the burgeoning capitalist class. The difference, as Marx saw it, was that communism, the new classless, stateless form of social and economic organization that would replace capitalism, represented the highest form of man's development.

At the time they were written Marx intended his analyses to apply only to the industrialized nations of western Europe, but in November 1917 the Bolsheviks, a communist party, took power in Russia. The triumph of the Bolsheviks was the culmination of the Russian Revolution, which had overthrown Tsar Nicholas II. By orthodox Marxist standards the

events in Russia made little sense. The nation's economy was essentially feudal, not capitalist, and was based on agriculture, not industry. Most of the population were peasants, not industrial workers, and the government was a hereditary autocracy, not a democracy. According to Marxist theory, Russia should have undergone capitalism and industrialization before a communist revolution occurred there.

But the Bolshevik leader Vladimir Lenin had modified Marxist thought by proposing that where conditions were not yet right for the communist revolution, as in Russia, the historical process could be sped up through the work of an elite, disciplined party of professional revolutionaries. This party would serve as the vanguard of consciousness of the proletariat. Using propaganda and political organization, the party would educate the workers about their situation and lead them to revolution. The success of the Bolsheviks in Russia seemed to verify Lenin's theories.

One can easily see the appeal that communism had for China's intellectuals. Here was a new, modern idea that promised rapid solutions for China's problems. It had not been discredited by events, as

Rebellious soldiers charge the Winter Palace of the tsar in Petrograd (St. Petersburg), Russia, in 1917. Many young, educated Chinese believed that the Russian Revolution, which overthrew Tsar Nicholas II and established a communist government, could serve as a model for change in their own country.

In 1923 the Soviet Union sent Mikhail Borodin (second from left) to reorganize Sun Yat-sen's *Guomindang* (Nationalist party) along Communist party lines. That same year Chiang (second from right) traveled to the Soviet Union, and his trip convinced him that the Soviets' willingness to aid the Guomindang masked territorial designs on China.

democracy seemed to have been. Indeed, recent events in Russia seemed to assert, the force of history was on its side. The Chinese were particularly drawn by Lenin's works on imperialism, which he deemed the highest stage of capitalism. The history of China during the past 120 years or so affirmed Lenin's thesis that the very nature of their economic system drove the capitalist nations to seek out colonies for economic exploitation. Patriotic Chinese also welcomed Lenin's announcement that he intended to renounce the Unequal Treaties and return any territory Russia had taken from China under the tsars.

Both Marx and Lenin held that the working class in each nation had the same primary interest in common — the overthrow of the bourgeoisie. Communism was therefore an international movement. In 1919 Lenin founded the Communist International, or Comintern, to direct and advise communist parties around the world. The Comintern directed immediate attention to China. The capitalist nations had proven themselves implacably hostile to communist government and had sent troops to the Soviet Union (as the Bolsheviks had renamed Russia) to aid opponents of the new regime. Although the Communists triumphed in the civil war that ensued, Lenin remained eager to establish friendly regimes on the Soviet Union's borders.

While the Comintern agent Adolph Joffe first tested the amenability of the warlord government in Beijing, the CCP was busy working among China's fledgling labor unions. Some industrialization had occurred since the fall of the Qings. In addition, many Chinese workers had gone to the European nations, particularly France, to serve as laborers during World War I and had thus been exposed to the ideas of the labor movement. The Communists succeeded in organizing unions in China's factories, where labor conditions during the 1920s were horrible. Workers were paid piecemeal wages for their labor during 12-hour days and were expected to be on the job 7 days a week. Child labor was common. In 1922 and 1923 there were major strikes by railway workers, seamen, and coal miners.

In early 1923 forces loyal to Sun recaptured Guangzhou, and Sun returned. Chiang remained in Shanghai. Sun was approached by Joffe, who offered to provide the Guomindang arms, money, and training if it were reorganized along Bolshevik party lines and admitted the CCP. Sun was hesitant but was reassured by Joffe's agreement that conditions in China were not right for the establishment of communism and that "the chief and immediate aim of China is the achievement of national union and national independence." Joffe also declared his allegiance to Sun's three principles. For years Sun had tried unsuccessfully to obtain aid from the Western nations; he readily agreed with Joffe that if the Guomindang were to achieve its goals it needed a more disciplined organization and a trained army. He also believed that he would be able to control the CCP members within the organization.

From the Communist point of view the merging of the CCP and the Guomindang was in keeping with Lenin's teaching that in semicolonial countries such as China the working-class party — the CCP — could temporarily join with bourgeois elements — the Guomindang — to achieve the overthrow of capitalist imperialism, at which point the Communists would shed their bourgeois allies. There was also an edge of hard practicality to the alliance. For all its early success, the CCP was still a small organization, and none of its leaders was as well known as Sun. Lenin had no doubts about the Comintern's ability to manipulate Sun, whom he said possessed "inimitable, one might say, virginal naivete." He sent Mikhail Borodin, an American-educated Comintern agent with previous experience in Mexico and Scotland, to direct the Guomindang's reorganization.

At the First Guomindang Congress, in January 1924, Sun endorsed cooperation with the Soviet Union, alliance with the CCP, and the development of mass movements among the workers as the Guomindang's new strategy. His trusted lieutenant Chiang was among those displeased with the new plans. Chiang had recently returned from the Soviet Union, where he had been dispatched by Sun. His

A woman member of the Guomindang explains its principles in early 1927, on the first leg of the northern expedition, undertaken by Chiang to defeat the warlords in the north and unify China under his leadership. With the death of Sun two years earlier, Chiang had assumed control of the Guomindang.

The Soongs were one of China's wealthiest and most powerful families. Despite frequent quarrels with Chiang, T. V. Soong (left) served two terms as his minister of finance and in other governmental positions. His sister Ching-ling married Sun Yat-sen and broke with Chiang after his purge of the Communists in 1927.

trip had convinced him that the Bolsheviks were not to be trusted. They intended to make the CCP their "chosen instrument," he wrote, in order to further their designs on Chinese territory. Chiang acknowledged that the Russians and Chinese Communists might be temporarily useful in ending Western imperialism, but he did not believe the alliance could be maintained for long.

Although Sun was disturbed by Chiang's misgivings, he appointed Chiang head of the Guomindang's new military academy at Huangpu. The academy was crucial to Sun's plans; from it was to come the trained army that would march against the northern warlords. Chiang appointed a Russian general he had met on his trip, Vasili Bluecher, as the academy's chief of staff. The cadets received political indoctrination as well as military training. Among the CCP members who served as political commissars was Zhou Enlai, but Chiang also developed a cadre of soldiers loyal to him.

Chiang had been courting Mei-ling Soong since shortly after he took up with Ch'en Chieh-ju. Now he again called upon her brother T. V. to serve as finance minister for the Guomindang. In the next 2 years Soong initiated a series of taxes, founded the Central Bank of China, and raised revenues in Guangdong province from $8 million to $80 million, enabling Chiang to make plans for the long-awaited northern expedition. Half of the revenues raised in Guangdong were to be used to finance the campaign.

But before the expedition could get under way, Sun died, on March 12, 1925. Although ill with cancer he had gone to Beijing to confer with the warlord Feng Yuxiang, called the Christian General, who was temporarily in control of the capital. Despite his request that his body be returned to the original republican capital of Nanjing for burial, he was interred at Beijing. The struggle for power among Sun's potential successors that ensued was paralleled by rifts within the Guomindang along the lines of degree of support for the alliance with the Communists. Liao Chung-k'ai headed the left group (those who most strongly favored the alliance),

Wang Ching-wei the centrists, and Hu Han-min the rightists. No one was certain where Chiang stood; although Sun had known of his mistrust of the Communists, he was generally regarded as a leftist. Chiang was not regarded seriously as a successor, primarily because unlike Sun, Liao, Hu, and Wang, he was not from Guangdong.

In July Wang was elected chairman of the Guomindang State Council. Liao's assassination shortly after seemed to cement Wang's accession, but Chiang's control of the army made him indispensable, which he proved by dealing the rebellious forces of the Hakka General a final defeat in October. By the end of the year Chiang was effectively in control of the Guomindang.

Chiang was ready to leave on the northern expedition in early 1926, but he still faced opposition from the Guomindang's Central Committee, where 7 of the 36 members, including Mao Zedong, were Communists. In March, claiming that a Communist plot to seize control of the Guomindang was afoot, Chiang proclaimed martial law in Guangzhou and arrested 25 prominent Communists, including Zhou Enlai. A short time later he established new policies designed to limit the power and activities of the CCP members within the Guomindang.

The catafalque containing the remains of Sun Yat-sen is borne from Beijing to Nanjing in May 1929. Sun's last wish was to be buried on the Purple Mountain at Nanjing, but his body rested for nearly four years at Beijing while Chiang's government constructed a huge mausoleum in his honor.

Soviet advisers with Chinese Communist troops in February 1927, not long after the fall of Hangchow to the Guomindang. The tenuous alliance between the Guomindang, the CCP, and the Soviets was still in place, but there were already indications that Chiang was planning to strike against the Communists.

Chiang's actions surprised the Soviets, who had told the Christian General that they believed Chiang to be the truest revolutionary among the Guomindang. They also surprised Wang, who resigned his posts and went into exile in Paris.

Chiang recognized that he would still need Soviet assistance if the northern expedition was to succeed, particularly because the Beijing government continued to receive aid from the West. He assured the Soviets that his actions had been directed only at certain disloyal individuals and not at the alliance with the Communists. At the direction of Joseph Stalin, who had succeeded Lenin, the CCP maintained the alliance. In June the Guomindang armies moved north, accompanied by CCP and Soviet political commissars.

The 5 most important northern warlords commanded more than 700,000 troops among them. Chiang led only 85,000 men, but the warlords were disorganized and more accustomed to betraying one another than uniting against a common enemy. The Christian General and Yen Hsi-shan, the "model" warlord of Shanxi, went over to Chiang in September. Wu P'ei-fu, the master of Hubei and Henan, fell next. The Guomindang established its new capital and wintered at Wuhan. Hangchow fell in February, Shanghai on March 22, and Nanjing two days later.

Chiang's military success did not quiet his opponents within the Guomindang. He was still nominally accountable to the Central Committee, where his opponents now numbered 16 of the 36 members, including Sun's widow, Ching-ling Soong. In March a Central Committee resolution called Chiang a dictator and criticized him for bringing "corrupt elements," including "bureaucrats, merchants, and other opportunists," into the party. That same month Chiang gave a speech in which he took credit for bringing the Communists into the Guomindang but warned that they had reached "the zenith of their power and arrogance" and advised them "not to take advantage of their influence."

The fall of Shanghai had been hastened by the success of a general strike organized by the CCP. As armed CCP pickets patrolled the city in the early days of April, rumors spread that Chiang was planning an attack on the Communists. In Moscow, Stalin said, "We are told that Chiang Kai-shek is making ready to turn on us again. I know that he is playing a cunning game with us, but it is he that will be crushed. We shall squeeze him like a lemon and then be rid of him." In Shanghai, Chiang, using his Green Gang connections, was meeting with the city's bankers and merchants. The financiers and entrepreneurs had no objection to Chiang making himself the new warlord of China, but they feared a communist revolution above all things and were willing to pay to see that it never happened.

Guomindang troops march into Taian, in Shandong, on their way to Beijing in June 1928. With the capture of Beijing later that month and the declaration of loyalty from Zhang Xueliang, the Young Marshal, six months later, Chiang and the Guomindang claimed the allegiance of virtually all of China.

5

A Disease of the Skin

Early on the morning of April 12, 1927, armed Green Gang thugs, disguised as labor pickets, attacked CCP members throughout Shanghai. The assault took the CCP by surprise. When a general strike was held the next day in protest, Guomindang troops fired on the strikers. CCP members were arrested or executed in the streets. Zhou Enlai, who had directed the CCP's efforts, managed to escape, but the CCP organization in Shanghai was destroyed. Estimates of the casualties range from 300 to 5,000. In the next days similar purges took place in Guangdong, Guangxi, Fujian, Zhejiang, Jiangsu, Anhui, and Nanjing. Theodore White and Annalee Jacoby wrote that the campaign against the CCP was "savage and relentless. Within the areas that Chiang controlled, his police butchered Communist leaders; families of known Communist leaders were wiped out; students were watched and spied on, and possession of Communist literature was made a crime punishable by death."

The purge split the Guomindang. Chiang made his new capital at Nanjing, while the party's left wing, headed by Wang, remained at Wuhan and passed resolutions condemning Chiang for the

He [Chiang] always made it clear that in his order of military priorities, the Communists came first, the Japanese second.
—BRIAN CROZIER
British journalist

Chiang married Mei-ling Soong on December 1, 1927. The connection with the Soong family reinforced his standing as Sun Yat-sen's presumptive heir. The union also ensured his access to the Soong family coffers and provided Mei-ling with the power she craved.

A commercial section of old Shanghai. After his conquest of the city in March 1927 Chiang turned on his erstwhile Communist allies. Anywhere from several hundred to several thousand of them were killed in the savage street fighting that ensued. Similar massacres followed in other Chinese cities.

"massacre of the people and oppression of the Party." The split was mirrored within Chiang's own family. Writing from Moscow, where he had been sent for his education, Chiang's son Ching-kuo said, "Chiang Kai-shek was my father and a revolutionary friend. He has now become my enemy. A few days ago he died as a revolutionary and arose as a counterrevolutionary. He used fine words about the revolution, but at the most convenient opportunity he betrayed it."

The merchants who had paid Chiang to eliminate the CCP got more than they bargained for. In his novel *Man's Fate*, which dealt with the events in Shanghai, the esteemed French man of letters André Malraux wrote: "It's not because you pay [Chiang] that he is going to destroy the Communists; it's because he is going to destroy the Communists that you pay him." The Communists were on the run, but the merchants were still expected to pay. When they proved reluctant, Chiang resorted to extortion. Kidnapping, torture, and murder were the customary tools. In 1927 alone he wrung $50 million from Shanghai's bankers, merchants, and industrialists.

The left Guomindang tried to sustain the illusion that it was the true revolutionary government of China, but with the CCP cadres in flight and the announcement in June by the left's erstwhile ally, the Christian General, Feng Yuxiang, that he now owed his loyalty to Chiang, the left was powerless. Recognizing the hopelessness of the situation, Borodin returned to the Soviet Union in July. Chiang's resignation of all his party posts in August was intended to demonstrate to the left faction just how helpless they were without him. In December the remaining members of the Central Committee — many had fled—invited Chiang to return.

That same month Chiang secured his status as Sun's heir by marrying Mei-ling Soong. Sun's widow, Ching-ling, told the American correspondent Edgar Snow that the marriage was "opportunism on both sides, with no love involved." Mei-ling craved power and recognized that Chiang would likely be the next ruler of China. Chiang needed the finances and expertise that Mei-ling's brother T. V. and brother-in-law H. H. Kung could provide. He also recognized that at some point he might need the assistance of the West, and the American-educated, English-speaking Mei-ling could serve as his emissary. The Soongs were Methodists; Chiang agreed to take religious instruction and was baptized in the faith in 1930.

Chiang spent 1928 carrying out the second phase of the northern expedition. He took Beijing in June; when the Young Marshal, Zhang Xueliang, proclaimed Manchuria's allegiance to the Guomindang by raising the Nationalist flag over Mukden in December, Chiang could claim control of a united China. By early 1929 the Guomindang had established governmental structures and was collecting taxes in 22 provinces.

In its early days the Guomindang government organized ministries of finance, railways, and industry and bureaus of agricultural research and health.

Summary trials and street executions were commonplace during the Guomindang's purge of the Chinese Communists in 1927. Such was the unhappy fate of these CCP members in Guangzhou.

There was a central bank, and highways were built. The Guomindang announced that China was now in its period of "political tutelage"; there were no popular elections, and no mention was made of how long the tutelage period was to last. As Sun had envisioned, the Guomindang set up five *yuan*, or councils, responsible for legislation, executive control, the judiciary, censorship, and examinations. As president of the state council and commander in chief of the military, Chiang possessed the ultimate power in the government. His colleagues said that he was "arrogant and conceited" and "uninhibitedly practicing dictatorship."

The main problem the new government faced was that its control was often only nominal. The warlords had not been vanquished but had merely proclaimed their loyalty to the new government. Like Zhang Xueliang in Manchuria, they had been allowed to remain in place in exchange for declarations of allegiance. In 1929 the new government had 2 million men under arms; they ate up 87 percent of the budget, leaving little available for industrialization or rural reconstruction. Most of these men belonged to the warlords' armies. When Chiang proposed disbanding most of the forces and using the troops as a labor corps for highway construction

Rice had been China's most important food crop for centuries, and it remained so during the Guomindang era, particularly in the south. Chiang's refusal to implement authentic land reform measures alienated the peasantry and left it receptive to the message of Mao Zedong and the CCP.

and mining projects, the warlords refused, recognizing that their armies were their only source of strength. As a result, Chiang was intermittently at war with Feng and other mutinous warlords throughout 1929 and 1930.

Chiang also faced new challenges from the Communists. After the massacre at Shanghai the CCP leadership, following instructions from Moscow, had attempted to foment revolts in several cities in the fall of 1927. Mao Zedong had opposed the plan but had reluctantly complied with orders. When the Autumn Harvest Uprisings were smashed, Mao retreated with 400 men to Jinggangshan, a mountainous region between Jiangxi and Hunan, where he formed the nucleus of what would become known as the Red Army.

From peasant stock himself, Mao had been studying conditions in China and had concluded that it was the peasantry that constituted China's true revolutionary force. He believed that the CCP and the Comintern had erred in emphasizing work among the proletariat, which in China was just too small to carry out a revolution. Forced to farm small plots rented at exorbitant rates from the gentry, it was the peasantry that was the exploited class. In his 1927 "Report on an Investigation into the Peasant Movement in Hunan," Mao wrote: "The present upsurge of the peasant movement is a colossal event. In a very short time . . . several hundred million peasants will rise like a mighty storm, like a hurricane, a force so swift and violent that no power, however great, will be able to hold it back. They will smash all the trammels that bind them and rush forward along the road to liberation. They will sweep all the imperialist warlords, corrupt officials, local tyrants, and evil gentry into their graves." In the Communist areas of Jiangxi and Hunan the peasants, aided by Mao's forces, seized land from the rich landlords and divided it among themselves. The Communists allowed the peasants to own the land individually; the implementation of the Communist goal of communal ownership was saved for a later date. The Communists encouraged the peasants to

Guomindang troops during the northern expedition. At the end of the campaign Chiang's program for disbanding China's armies was rejected by the recently vanquished warlords.

dispense a rough "revolutionary justice"; landlords were killed or beaten. When the gentry screamed that the peasant violence constituted a reign of terror, Mao wrote that it was "necessary to create terror for a while in every rural area; otherwise it would be impossible to suppress the activities of the counter-revolutionaries in the countryside or overthrow the gentry." The CCP cadres and Red Army soldiers maintained a strict discipline and were instructed to do everything possible to win the support of the peasantry. By 1931 the CCP controlled a good portion of Jiangxi and was steadily expanding its influence.

The Guomindang had written land reform legislation, but it was never enacted. Chiang's government relied on the support of businessmen, financiers, and the rural gentry, none of whom were interested in a redistribution of China's wealth. To the peasantry, Chiang's government was no different from those that had preceded it. White and Jacoby wrote that "looking up at his government from below, the peasant could see no change. His taxes ran on as before; his rent and interest rates were just as high as ever; his court of appeal consisted of the same men who had always denied his demands. The revolution had brought him nothing."

The Japanese invaded Manchuria in September 1931, but Chiang advised the Young Marshal to do nothing. He was busy directing his third bandit-suppression campaign against the Communists in Jiangxi. Although the Guomindang forces greatly outnumbered the Communists, the Red Army used Mao's four rules of guerrilla warfare — the enemy advances, we retreat; the enemy halts and encamps, we harass; the enemy seeks to avoid battle, we attack; the enemy retreats, we pursue — to prevail. While the Japanese consolidated their hold on northern China and established the puppet state of Manchukuo, Chiang's third and fourth campaigns ended in failure.

Chiang was unable to see that the ultimate unification of China depended as much on the support of the people as on force of arms. In November and December of 1931, 70,000 students rioted in Bei-

Inhabitants of the walled city of Mukden, where the Japanese began their invasion of Manchuria in September 1931. Chiang advised Manchuria's warlord, Zhang Xueliang, not to resist the Japanese, even though Zhang's forces greatly outnumbered theirs.

jing, demanding that Chiang fight the Japanese, but he took no action. When the Changjiang River flooded at about the same time, killing 2 million people, the government failed to provide adequate relief for the thousands left homeless, starving, or infected with cholera, typhoid, or dysentery. Although Chiang spoke periodically of abrogating the Unequal Treaties and expelling the Westerners, no action was taken. More indicative of his government's stance were his pledge to protect private property and the execution of 50 soldiers who took part in anti-Western rioting.

With T. V. Soong as finance minister, the Shanghai bankers had been forced to buy millions of dollars worth of government bonds. Although the practice strengthened the ties between the Guomindang and the financiers, the government was run on a sound financial basis, and in 1932 Soong succeeded in balancing the budget. In 1933 the brothers-in-law broke over Soong's insistence that Chiang fight the Japanese. Soong was succeeded by H. H. Kung, who immediately announced that suppression of the Communists was more important than a balanced budget. The government continued to extort money from the banks — money that should have gone for agricultural or industrial development — resulting in a severe recession from 1933 to 1935, followed by horrendous inflation. In 1934 a law was passed requiring savings banks to invest one-quarter of their assets in government bonds. The following year Chiang brought five of China's largest banks under his personal control. The Bank of England's representative in China, Cyril Rogers, said that Kung had the mentality of a 12 year old and asserted that if his conversations with Kung about banking were tape-recorded and played abroad, Chiang's government would become an international laughingstock. Kung responded to each new fiscal crisis by raising taxes or simply having more money printed, measures that Chiang readily endorsed. After 1935 the government no longer bothered publishing a budget or recording its expenditures.

The Guomindang had an additional source of revenue. The Green Gang's control of the opium trade soon became a government monopoly that was extended to heroin and morphine. Peasants told of being forced by government soldiers to plant opium instead of food crops. By 1937 more than 85 percent of the world's heroin supply was coming from China. Many packages bore the official imprint of Chiang's National Anti-Opium Bureau.

Chiang launched his fifth and final bandit-suppression campaign in October 1933. Following

From Manchuria the Japanese extended their control to the province of Jehol and installed Pu-yi as the emperor of a puppet state called Manchukuo. This photo shows Japanese forces on the move in Jehol in the winter of 1933.

strategy devised by a German military adviser, General Hans von Seecht, the army built hundreds of miles of military supply roads around the Communist strongholds in Jiangxi, Hunan, Fujian, Guangdong, and Guangxi. Blockhouses were built, and an economic blockade was imposed. As the army advanced the circle tightened, and the process was repeated. All told, 900,000 Guomindang troops, supported by 400 airplanes, took part. One year later the Communists found themselves virtually surrounded and decided to abandon their hard-won territory in the south. Thus began the Long March, a 6,000-mile retreat that proved a marvel of military tactics, daring, and stamina. Under the leadership of Mao and Zhu De, the Red Army's guerrillas eluded and outfought Chiang's unwieldy divisions and traversed China's most rugged terrain to safety in Shaanxi. They marched through 11 provinces, crossed 18 mountain chains, forded 24 rivers, fought 10 warlords, and temporarily took 62 cities. Fewer than 10,000 of the more than 100,000 who started the journey survived the yearlong ordeal, but the Long March was judged a Communist victory. Their survival was deemed a miracle and gave the Red Army an aura of invincibility. While Chiang's troops killed nearly 950,000 peasants during the course of the fifth bandit-suppression campaign, the Communists won new supporters among the rural poor with their promises of land reform, and the people of the north embraced the Red Army's promise that it would lead resistance against the Japanese.

Chiang responded by cracking down on dissent. Critics of his regime had always been liable to arrest by the secret police. In 1933 six of the country's foremost writers, including Feng Kung, widely regarded as China's preeminent woman author, were arrested, forced to dig a ditch, bound, tossed in, and buried alive. Now the repression became more widespread. Those who spoke out against the government were labeled communists, arrested, and often executed. At the end of 1935, 7 leaders of the National Salvation Movement, which preached resistance to Japan, were jailed, and 14 magazines

As the Red Army passed through Guizhou province on the Long March, its constant feints and changes of direction kept Chiang's forces off balance. At Loushan Pass (pictured), 40 miles north of the city of Zunyi, Communist forces under Peng Dehuai routed two of Chiang's divisions, inflicting severe casualties.

Survivors of the Long March pose in Shaanxi. Although Chiang had succeeded in driving the Communists from their bases in the south, the Communists won new followers on the course of their 6,000-mile trek by advocating land reform and promising to lead the fight against the Japanese.

with anti-Japanese editorial policies were shut down. The suppression drove many Chinese, particularly students and intellectuals, to support the CCP.

Chiang sought to counter the CCP's ideology with one of his own. He watched with approval as the Nazi Adolf Hitler rode a program of racism, nationalism, militarism, and anticommunism to power in Germany. In 1934 Chiang launched the New Life Movement, an amalgam of Confucianism and Nazi-style fascism. Its motto was "propriety, justice, honesty, and self-respect." Chiang urged his nation to emulate Germany, which had recovered from its defeat in World War I, paid off the reparations exacted by the victorious Allies, and renounced what it regarded as unfair treaties forced upon it. He developed an elite force known as the Blueshirts, most of whom were graduates of the military academy at Huangpu. The Blueshirts' slogan was "nationalize, militarize, productivize," and they were the sworn enemy of Western liberalism. They attacked Chinese in Western-style dress, poured acid on patrons of Western movies, and enforced the New Life Movement's 4 virtues, 8 principles, and 95 rules of daily behavior, which included such admonitions as stand up straight, button your clothes, eat quietly, wash your face in cold water, and do not spit heedlessly. Chinese were warned of the evils of drinking, gambling, dancing, smoking, and Western-style hairdos. Chiang said that the New Life Movement's goal was to "militarize the lives of the citizens of the entire nation so that they can cultivate courage and swiftness, the endurance of suffering and a tolerance for hard work, and especially the habit and ability of unified action, so that they will at any time sacrifice for the nation." The New Life Movement, Chiang wrote, would bring an end to "drift and insipidity," which expressed themselves in "acts which do not distinguish between good and evil, right and wrong, and private interests and public welfare. Hence, our officials are hypocritical, greedy, and corrupt, our people are disorganized and indifferent to the welfare of the nation; our youths are degenerate and irresponsible."

While the Chinese were demonstrating an essential indifference to the New Life Movement, the Japanese extended their influence from Manchuria to Shandong, Hebei, Shanxi, and part of Inner Mongolia throughout 1935. With the Communists encouraging resistance, massive demonstrations for national salvation took place in Beijing in December and soon spread to Hangchow, Shanghai, Wuhan, Changsha, and Wuchow. Still believing that his forces could not move against the Japanese until they were stronger and the Communists had been eliminated, Chiang laid plans for his sixth bandit-suppression campaign. In December 1936 he flew to Xian to enlist the support of Zhang Xueliang for his newest offensive against the Communists. Zhang believed that the Japanese constituted a more immediate danger to China, and he was frustrated by Chiang's indifference to that threat. He took Chiang captive, releasing him only when he agreed to head a united front with the Communists for the national salvation of China.

6

Space for Time

On the night of July 7, 1937, a dispute over a missing Japanese soldier escalated into full-scale fighting between Japanese and Chinese forces near the Marco Polo Bridge, not far from Beijing. Chiang had 1.7 million men with which to combat the Japanese. The Red Army was also poised for resistance. Although Chiang had finally been convinced to form a united front, the alliance between the Guomindang and the CCP was tenuous at best. The CCP had offered to end land confiscations, hold elections, and place the Red Army under Chiang's command if he agreed to end the civil war, release political prisoners, guarantee freedom of speech, and lead the war against Japan. Chiang responded by demanding that the CCP dismantle its soviets — workers' and peasants' councils that functioned as local governments — and renounce the theory and practice of class struggle. No agreement was reached; the united front was therefore essentially an informal truce between the two parties based on the mutual need for cooperation in combatting Japan.

Both sides were motivated by expediency and self-interest, as well as patriotism, in forming the united

> *He was to be the dominant figure in China, but never its unchallenged master.*
> —BRIAN CROZIER
> British journalist
> on Chiang

The flag of the Chinese Communists flies above a Red Army machine gunner combatting the Japanese in 1937. That year the Japanese attempted to extend their control from Manchuria to all of China, initiating a war that would last for the next eight years.

front. Chiang had recognized, albeit somewhat belatedly, that the nation wanted him to fight the Japanese. By leading the war of resistance, Chiang would gain new support for his government. In the early days of the war China finally achieved the unity that had eluded it for so many years. The abuses of Chiang's government were forgotten. White and Jacoby observed that "the war against Japan made Chiang Kai-shek almost a demigod. For a brief moment at the war's outbreak he stood as the incarnate symbol of all China's will to resistance and freedom." The crisis even provoked his son Ching-kuo to return from the Soviet Union and reconcile with his father. The united front was also essential for Chiang because he was dependent on the Soviet Union for arms and money to conduct the war of resistance. Despite Japanese provocation, both the United States and Great Britain were not yet willing to involve themselves in a war in Asia; both were hoping to delay involvement in what appeared to be an inevitable armed conflict in Europe. Chiang had been friendly with the Germans, but Hitler was now courting the Japanese and had recalled his advisers from China. Only the Soviets were willing to aid Chiang. They sent him weapons, aircraft, pilots, and military advisers. Stalin sent $250 million worth of aid in the first 2 years of the war, along with a message to Chiang that "if he wants to do away with any manifestations of disloyalty on the part of his people while the fight continues, he should arrange to shoot at least 4.5 million people."

The Communists recognized that the role they played in eliminating the Japanese would be crucial to their future success. Many Chinese, particularly in the north, supported the CCP because it was the party of resistance. The CCP knew that Japan's defeat could propel them to power in China after the war. A 1937 CCP resolution said that "force being the determining factor in China's politics, emphasis should be put on expanding the Communist Party's armed forces in the course of resistance to lay the foundation in the struggle for political power in the future." Mao realized the war would offer the CCP an opportunity to extend its influence. The

CCP's policy would be "70 percent expansion, 20 percent dealing with the Guomindang, and 10 percent resisting Japan," he said. This policy would be carried out in three stages. The first would be "outward cooperation" with the Guomindang, serving as "camouflage" for party work. The second would be "contending" with the Guomindang for control north of the Huanghe River. In the final stage the Red Army would "penetrate deeply into Central China" and "wrest the leadership from the hands of the Guomindang."

The Japanese forces advanced rapidly. Beijing and Tianjin fell almost immediately. Chiang was willing to abandon the north to the invaders and make his stand at the Changjiang River in defense of Shanghai, where the fierce resistance they encountered from August to November 1937 greatly surprised the Japanese. The Chinese inflicted 60,000 casualties on the invaders, but they lost several hundred thousand men themselves and were forced to withdraw. Chiang's government and the main body of his troops retreated 600 miles west along the Changjiang to Hankow (now part of Wuhan) while the Japanese took Nanjing. The fall of the former Guomindang capital in December was accompanied by an orgy of looting, murder, rape, and other atrocities by the Japanese. Several hundred thousand civilians were killed.

The rape of Nanjing was intended to terrorize China into immediate surrender, but Chiang did

Chinese soldiers at the Marco Polo Bridge near Beijing. The disappearance of a single Japanese soldier during skirmishing between Chinese and Japanese forces stationed near the bridge on the night of July 7, 1937, formed the pretext for more extensive Japanese aggression against China.

A poster displayed in Nanjing in December 1937 urges resistance to Japan. It portrays a Chinese soldier vaulting the Great Wall to carry the fight to the Japanese in the north. The Chinese characters read "Recover lost territories, relieve our Manchurian countrymen." That same month the Japanese overran Nanjing and committed countless atrocities against its inhabitants.

not intend to capitulate. He told the *New York Times* immediately after Shanghai's fall that "the enemy never realizes that China's territory is not conquerable. She is indestructible. As long as there is one spot in China free from enemy encroachment, the National Government will remain supreme." When Shanghai was evacuated, 14,000 tons of industrial equipment were loaded onto rowboats, which were camouflaged and then poled up the Changjiang to Chongqing, in Szechuan, where it was reassembled. Machinery from the huge Yufeng textile mill —8,000 tons worth—was first carried by rail to Hankow. When Hankow fell in October 1938, the equipment was put aboard 380 junks for transportation to Chongqing. All but 21 of the junks made it through the Changjiang's treacherous narrows. Similar operations took place in northern and central China throughout 1938 and 1939. Steel mills, textile plants, and munitions factories were moved in this fashion. The nation's universities underwent a similar migration. In 1938, 94 of China's 108 colleges were forced to close or move inland, but by the next year most were open and functioning again, and enrollment actually rose 25 percent in the autumn of 1939.

After Nanjing, Chiang went briefly on the offensive. Guomindang troops under Li Tsung-jen defeated the Japanese at Taierchuang, on the southern Shandong Peninsula, in April 1938, but it was to be the only Nationalist victory of the war. As the Chinese forces withdrew through Henan they dynamited the dikes of the Huanghe. The maneuver succeeded in slowing the Japanese advance, but it also flooded 3 provinces, 11 cities, and 4,000 villages and left 2 million people homeless.

During his study of military history Chiang had paid particular attention to the French emperor Napoleon Bonaparte's campaign in Russia in 1812. The Russians had prevailed over the superior French forces by using their country's massive size, geography, and harsh winter climate against the invaders. As the French advanced, the Russians withdrew into the interior, drawing the French after them. The French supply lines became overextended and were easy prey for the marauding Russian cavalry. The Russians practiced a "scorched earth policy," burning crops and fields behind them so the French could not live off the land. Even the city of Moscow was burned shortly after the French occupied it. With the coming of winter, the French retreated, but the demoralized and ill-provisioned Grande Armée was now an easy target for Russian hit-and-run raids, and Napoleon's army was devastated before it could reach the Russian border.

Chiang believed a similar strategy could work in China, a vast country full of such protective natural barriers as rivers and mountain ranges. The demolition of the Huanghe dikes marked the initial implementation of his scorched earth policy. After Taierchuang and the fall of Hankow and Guangzhou in October 1938, Chiang withdrew to Chongqing,

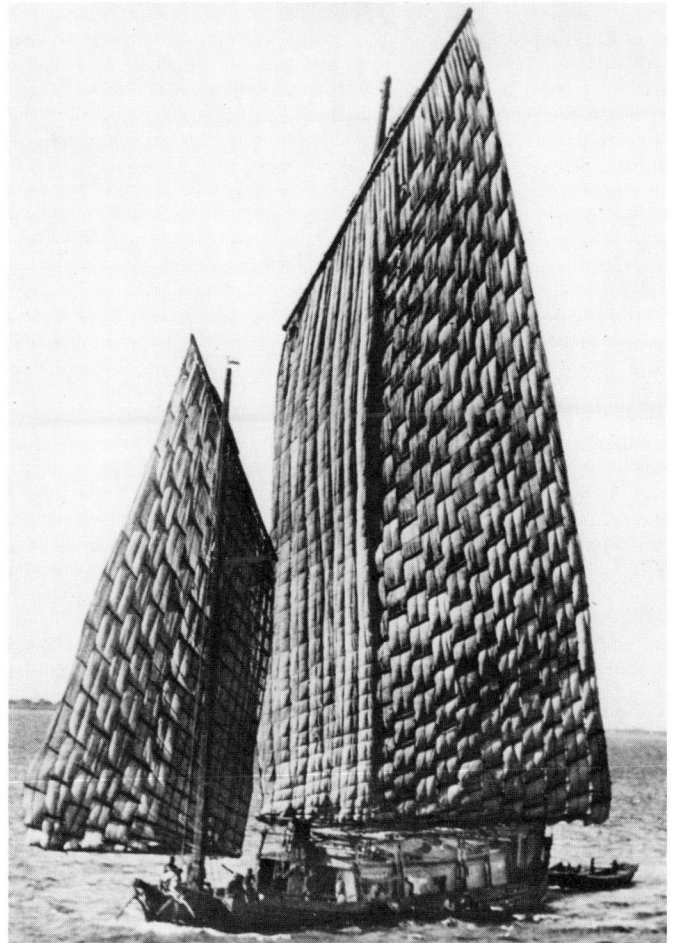

A junk on the Changjiang (Yangtze) River, of the type used to transport industrial equipment and machinery from the coastal cities inland, so as to avoid its capture by the Japanese. Junks were the standard vessels used by Chinese on their waterways and the high seas.

Japanese soldiers attempting to bridge this stream in northern China were sent scurrying when the Chinese ignited the sorghum fields surrounding it. Chiang burned crops and demolished dikes to slow the Japanese advance and make it difficult for them to live off the land.

where he made his new capital. From Chongqing Chiang said that he was trading space for time, that although the Japanese controlled the coasts, much of the interior, and all of the major cities, China could not be conquered. For the next six years the war in China was essentially a stalemate, graphically described by White and Jacoby: "This China War was fought along a flexible belt of no man's land, fifty to a hundred miles deep, all up and down the middle of China. In this belt of devastation the Chinese had destroyed every road, bridge, railway, or ferry that might aid the Japanese in one of their periodic thrusts; the only Chinese offense was to reduce the country to immobility. Japanese and Chinese troops chased each other across the belt for six years; the peasants died, the troops bled, the villages were burned to the ground, towns changed hands as many as six or seven times, and yet for six years the front remained stable with few significant changes."

Chiang's strategy was based in part on his growing certainty that Japan's expansionism would ultimately force the United States to take action against it, but he was unable to see what it cost him in popular support. Not enamored with the Guomindang to begin with, the peasants resented having their crops and homes burned or flooded, and Chiang's withdrawal seemed like abandonment. The nation had united behind Chiang as a symbol of resistance, but he was in Chongqing while the majority of his countrymen were under Japanese occupation. At the same time, from their base in Yanan, the Communists were laying the foundation for future expansion. In the areas under its control the CCP emphasized lowering taxes and rent rather than the radical land reform practiced earlier. The Red Army carried out offensives against the Japanese, and the CCP organized an active guerrilla resistance movement among the peasantry.

Chongqing had been a small provincial trading center, but during the war years its population increased fivefold, to upward of 1 million, and the town was transformed into what the writer Brooks Atkinson called "a witches' fairground of anxieties, suspicions and intrigue." While the city endured daily bombing raids, Chiang directed his government from the three homes he had commandeered. Believing U.S. involvement inevitable, he refused to order his forces to attack. Rampaging inflation continued to devastate the economy. Prices increased 49 percent in 1938, 83 percent in 1939, 124 percent in 1940, 173 percent in 1941, and 235 percent in 1945. The Soviet Union signed a neutrality pact with Japan in 1940, meaning that Chiang no longer received supplies from Stalin. In July of that same year the British gave in to Japanese pressure and closed the Burma Road, which had been Chongqing's only supply artery. The Japanese installed Chiang's old rival Wang Ching-wei as head of the puppet government they established in occupied China. Despite the setbacks, Chiang refused to consider Japanese peace proposals.

The Communists were more successful. The Red Army was divided into the Eighth Route Army, which operated north of the Changjiang, and the New Fourth Army, which operated in the south. Boosted by peasant recruits, membership in the Eighth Route Army grew from 45,000 to 400,000 from 1937 to 1940, and the New Fourth Army grew from 15,000 to 100,000 during that same period. Chiang wanted to restrict Communist influence to the north, and in January 1941 his 40th Division clashed with the New Fourth Army near Shanghai. Casualties were heavy, and the fighting brought an end to the united front.

On December 7, 1941, the Japanese air force attacked the U.S. military installation at Pearl Harbor, Hawaii, and the United States entered the war against Japan, which was merely one theater in a global conflict — World War II — that saw the United States, France, Great Britain, and the Soviet Union allied against Germany and Italy in Europe and Great Britain and the United States joined against Japan in the Pacific. Chiang had been eagerly awaiting what he regarded as an inevitable conflict between the United States and Japan and welcomed the American entrance into the war as China's salvation. He was named supreme allied commander of the China-Burma-India theater of war by U.S. president Franklin Roosevelt. An American general, Joseph Stilwell, was dispatched to serve as his chief of staff. Stilwell was to command all U.S. forces in China and supervise the distribution of U.S. aid.

Blunt and acidic, Stilwell was a self-proclaimed "old China hand" who had spent years in the country, spoke the language, and believed he understood the nation and its people. Chiang resented his presence from the outset. Chiang could not understand why he needed Stilwell's approval for expenditures of U.S. aid — distributed under a program known as Lend-Lease — when the other Allies were allowed to spend their Lend-Lease dollars as they saw fit. Stilwell was appalled by the corruption of Chiang's government. Generals routinely diverted weaponry and matériel intended for their troops into their own private warehouses and sold it to the Japanese. Casualties went unreported and troop strength was exaggerated so that officers could pocket pay for

wounded, dead, or nonexistent soldiers. Government ministers made fortunes speculating in American dollars on the black market. Troops went into battle unfed and unequipped.

At the heart of the conflict between Chiang and Stilwell was the Chinese leader's refusal to order his troops on the offensive. Chiang made his position clear: "For me, the big problem is not Japan, but the unification of my country. I am sure that you Americans are going to beat the Japanese some day, with or without the help of the troops I am holding back for use against the Communists in the northwest. On the other hand, if I let Mao Zedong push his propaganda against all of free China, we run the risk — and so do all of you Americans — of winning for nothing." At another point he said, "The Japanese are a disease of the skin. The Communists are a disease of the heart."

After the fall of Nanjing in December 1937 Chiang made his new capital at Chongqing. Japanese bombers pounded the city almost daily, and a steady influx of refugees increased the city's population fivefold during the war years.

General Joseph Stilwell, shown here conferring with the Guomindang general Liao Yao-hsuang, prided himself on his knowledge of the Chinese people, culture, and language. At the outbreak of World War II U.S. president Franklin Roosevelt sent Stilwell to serve as Chiang's chief of staff, but the two men did not get along.

In order to boost Chinese morale, Britain and the United States announced in October 1942 that they were renouncing the Unequal Treaties. The following year Madame Chiang traveled to the United States, where she received a great deal of favorable publicity, particularly in Henry Luce's publications. The publisher of *Time* and *Fortune* magazines, Luce had grown up in China, where his parents were Presbyterian missionaries, and since the 1930s he had been lauding Chiang and the Soong family as the symbols of a progressive, Western-oriented, anticommunist China. In November 1943 Chiang met with Roosevelt and Prime Minister Winston Churchill of Great Britain at Cairo, Egypt, where Roosevelt promised to arm and train 90 Chinese divisions and restore all territory seized from China by the Japanese.

Roosevelt's promises were designed to win further cooperation from Chiang, but they went unfulfilled and Chiang remained intransigent. Although in a fit of rage he might beat a general who mistreated conscripts or order the head of the selective service shot, Chiang was unable or unwilling to take steps to halt the abuses by his government. The rich were allowed to buy their way out of military service, whereas peasants were kidnapped from their villages and impressed into the armed forces. Unwilling conscripts were often roped together like draft animals. By 1943 the Guomindang army was, in Stilwell's words, "unpaid, unfed, shot with sickness and starvation." There was no medical care. Soldiers suffered from typhoid, influenza, dysentery, malaria, scabies, and beri-beri. Up to 15 percent of the men in a typical division suffered from tuberculosis. Those lucky enough to get paid found their wages made valueless by inflation. In 1943 a major in the Chinese army was paid the equivalent of $60 a month, but a pair of shoes cost $1,200.

Chiang met with Roosevelt (center) and Prime Minister Winston Churchill of Great Britain in Cairo, Egypt, in November 1943 to discuss strategy for the Asian war. Chiang believed the conference confirmed his status as a major world leader, but the promises Roosevelt made to him there to commit more arms and attention to the war in China went unfulfilled.

A famished Chinese boy from Hunan carries his starving mother to a refugee camp administered by the United Nations. Famine was widespread in China during the war years because of Chiang's scorched earth policy, the Guomindang's seizure of crops in payment for taxes, the privations of the Japanese, and the destruction of land and crops in battle.

Nor was starvation confined to the military. Ten to 15 million peasants starved to death during the war with Japan. In 1943 and 1944 Henan province was racked by famine caused when the Guomindang confiscated an entire year's grain crop as taxes. Three million people died; another 3 million became refugees. By 1944 even the middle class was finding it difficult to obtain sufficient food, and there were riots and uprisings in Guizhou, Gansu, Fujien, Hubei, and Szechuan.

While Chiang surrounded himself with the trappings of power — he held 82 titles during the war years — Stilwell was recommending that the United States increase aid to the Communists, who were willing to fight, and merge the CCP and Guomindang forces. He wrote that Chiang was unable to see that "the mass of the Chinese people welcome the Reds as being the only visible hope of relief from crushing taxation, the abuses of the Army. . . . Under Chiang they now begin to see what they may expect. Greed, corruption, favoritism, more taxes, a ruined currency ." His assessment was echoed by U.S. vice-president Henry Wallace and various State Department officials, who visited Yanan and concluded that the Communists were more agrarian democrats than hard-core Marxist-Leninists.

With the steady U.S. advance across the Pacific threatening their home islands, the Japanese launched a major offensive in China in the spring of 1944. The Guomindang forces were mauled. They lost more than 700,000 men and 100,000 square miles of territory. Roosevelt wired Chiang in July that Stilwell was to replace him as the supreme commander of the allied forces in China, including the Communists. Chiang simply refused to be relieved. Roosevelt recognized that Chiang and Stilwell could no longer work together and was unwilling to risk Chiang's permanent enmity at such a critical juncture of the war. In October 1944 he recalled Stilwell.

Chinese refugees from the Shandong Peninsula huddled aboard the deck of a steamship making its way into the harbor at Lü-ta (Dairen). Although Lü-ta was in Japanese-controlled Manchuria, it offered a sanctuary from the fighting that ravaged central and southern China from 1937 to 1945.

7

Heaven Sees as the People See

With an Allied victory in Europe all but inevitable, Roosevelt, Churchill, and Stalin met in February 1945 at Yalta, on the Black Sea in the Soviet Union, to discuss postwar arrangements. Although Japan was reeling — it had lost most of its Pacific island possessions, was being pounded daily by U.S. bombing raids, and its economy was in a shambles — Roosevelt still thought it likely that an invasion of the Japanese home islands would be necessary to force a surrender and wanted the Soviet Union's assistance. In exchange for Stalin's assurance that the Soviet Union would enter the Pacific war two or three months after Germany's surrender, Roosevelt promised that at war's end the Soviet Union would obtain control of the former Chinese possessions of the Kurile Islands, Outer Mongolia, and south Sakhalin. The Soviets were also granted jurisdiction over the ports and railroads in Manchuria.

Chiang was angered by China's exclusion from the conference. Even though Stalin swore Roosevelt to secrecy regarding the agreements, rumors about their content soon reached Chiang. He regarded the Yalta accords as evidence that the Western nations were no more committed to preserving China's sov-

> *[Chiang was] a man ripped out of the old world too soon, plunged into a new world he could not understand.*
> —THEODORE WHITE
> American historian

In his 1949 New Year's Day address Chiang threatened to resign, but the gesture was an empty one. The civil war with the Communists had resumed at the end of World War II, and by January 1949 Chiang's military forces had been mauled and his government was on the verge of collapse.

The United States dropped the atomic bomb on Hiroshima, Japan, on August 6, 1945, leaving the city little but rubble and burned-out remains. Three days later a second bomb was dropped on the city of Nagasaki. The devastation helped induce Japan's surrender.

ereignty and territorial integrity than they ever had been. The development of the atomic bomb by the United States and its use against the Japanese cities of Hiroshima and Nagasaki in August 1945 made an invasion of Japan unnecessary. Japan surrendered on August 14, but Soviet troops had already moved into Manchuria. Chiang had no choice but to order his foreign minister to negotiate a treaty with Stalin. The resulting agreement gave Port Arthur to the Soviets, made Lü-ta (Dairen) a free city, allowed the Soviets to hold elections in Outer Mongolia to determine its future status, and provided for joint Sino-Soviet ownership of the Manchurian railways. Stalin agreed to recognize the Guomindang as China's national government and to refrain from interfering in China's internal affairs.

The growth of the CCP during the war years and its success in expanding the area under its control refuted Chiang's claim that the Guomindang was China's sole government. CCP membership had been 40,000 in 1937; at war's end it was 1.2 million. The CCP governed more than 250,000 square miles of territory and 35 million people. The Red Army had almost 500,000 regular troops and more than twice that many in guerrilla and militia units.

Two weeks after Japan's surrender, Mao and Chiang met at Chongqing. Mao distrusted Chiang and made the journey from Yanan only when his safety was guaranteed by U.S. envoy Patrick Hurley. U.S. policy was to encourage negotiation toward the formation of a coalition government that would incorporate both the CCP and the Guomindang while continuing to provide Chiang with military and financial support. Mao expressed willingness to share power and reduce his forces, but Chiang had no intention of allowing the CCP into the government. When the talks broke down after seven weeks, the civil war resumed, but skirmishing had begun even while Chiang and Mao were still negotiating.

Chiang seemed to have the advantage when the civil war began. He had 3 million troops at his command. The Japanese forces in Manchuria surrendered to the Soviets, who in turn passed the majority of the Japanese weaponry on to the Guomindang. The United States remained a generous source of aid for Chiang's government and gave Chiang more than $2 billion between 1945 and 1948. When the Soviets left Manchuria in March 1946, U.S. planes transported Chiang's well-equipped troops to the north.

The Soviet forces had stayed longer than the expected three months, however, and Chiang's troops found the Red Army already firmly in control of the Manchurian countryside. Taking no chances as to the eventual victor in the civil war, Stalin was cunningly supporting both sides and had allowed the Communists to establish themselves in Manchuria. Chiang protested loudly, but in November 1945 he had asked the Soviets to stay because his forces were not yet ready to occupy the rich northeastern provinces.

At the same time Chiang was managing to alienate what little popular support he still possessed. Asserting that any Chinese who had lived under Japanese control was a collaborator, Chiang gave his officials and generals free rein to loot and pillage in the newly liberated areas. Manchuria was hit particularly hard. The Soviets had begun by carrying off most of Manchuria's heavy industrial equipment, and the Guomindang soldiers and officials took everything else. While the Communists were implementing land reform in the rural areas under their control, Guomindang troops simply seized land that had been controlled by the Japanese during the war and refused to return it to the peasants.

Enthusiastic crowds greeted the U.S. Marines who liberated Tianjin from the Japanese in 1945. At war's end the Guomindang and CCP scrambled to place their forces in advantageous position for the postwar struggle for power.

CCP chairman Mao Zedong (left) and Chiang toast each other at a dinner in Chongqing in the autumn of 1945. U.S. diplomats arranged negotiations between the two in an attempt to forestall a resumption of the civil war, but the meetings were unsuccessful.

The ruinous inflation continued. Prices doubled 67 times between August 1945 and January 1946, then rose 85,000 times in the next 6 months. In Shanghai wholesale prices were seven times as high at the end of 1946 as they had been at the year's outset. In 1947 prices rose hourly while the living standard dropped by a third. Virtually all of the country's roadways and railways had been destroyed, making communication and transportation difficult if not impossible. Meanwhile, government officials grew rich from looting. Aid from the United States was stolen and converted into cash in the bank accounts of Guomindang officials, then invested abroad. Demonstrations against the government were harshly suppressed, and critics of the government were jailed.

The Communists found the military situation in Manchuria to their liking and were perfectly willing to allow Chiang temporary control of the cities. With the economy ruined, control of the countryside meant control of the food supply. The devastated transportation system made it difficult for Chiang to supply his troops. Although the Manchurian railway system had remained largely intact under Japanese control during the war, the Communists now concentrated their efforts on its destruction. The huge Guomindang garrisons were soon isolated in defensive positions in the cities, where they grew demoralized, and their rapaciousness and often brutal treatment of the citizenry increased popular resentment against Chiang's regime.

Guomindang morale sank even lower when in 1946 the United States declared an embargo on arms shipments to Chiang. State Department officials such as John Carter Vincent, John Payton Davies, and John Service were growing increasingly vociferous in their criticism of Chiang's government. The Guomindang, they charged, was hopelessly corrupt. It had lost the support of the people and could not possibly win the civil war, and U.S. interests would not be served by throwing more money after a losing cause. The Guomindang seemed to have won a great victory in March 1947 when its troops captured Yanan, but the Communists had willingly abandoned their capital in preparation for a huge spring offensive to be led by Lin Biao, whom the Communists boasted had never been defeated in battle.

A series of defeats left the government troops in Manchuria isolated in Lü-ta, Tsinan, Changchun, and Chilin (Kirin). While in China on a fact-finding mission in August, U.S. general Albert Wedemeyer, despite his anticommunist stance, strongly criticized the defeatism, lethargy, incompetence, mismanagement, greed, and corruption of Chiang's government. The Guomindang was now plagued by wholesale defection in the army and informants in the government. CCP leaders sometimes knew of the Guomindang's plans before its officials and generals did. By 1948 the Communist military forces, strengthened by Guomindang defections and successful recruiting among the peasantry, numbered 2 million.

Tsinan, then Lü-ta, then Changchun and the rest of Manchuria fell in the autumn of 1948. Chiang desperately pleaded for more aid. He again dispatched his wife to the United States, but her official welcome was less warm than it had been in the war years. (Harry Truman, who was then president, later dismissed the Soongs as "thieves. Every damn one of them.") General George Marshall, the architect of a plan for the economic reconstruction of

The Communist forces roll into Shanghai in May 1949. The banner portrays their leaders, Mao Zedong and Zhou Enlai. By this point Chiang was already preparing to move his government and armed forces to the island of Taiwan.

The Red Army entered Chiang's former capital at Nanjing in April 1949. Supplied with equipment captured from the Guomindang and supported by a friendly populace, the Communist soldiers were now much better provisioned than they had been at the beginning of the civil war. The tubelike sacks that some of the men are wearing over their shoulders contain rice.

Europe, told Congress that "the Chinese Communists have succeeded to a considerable extent in identifying their movement with the popular demand for change in present conditions. On the other hand, there have been no indications that the present Chinese government, with its traditions and methods, could satisfy the popular demand or create conditions which would satisfy the mass of the Chinese people and prevent further violence and civil disobedience." General David Barr, U.S. military adviser to Chiang, wrote that "military matériel and economic aid in my opinion is less important to the salvation of China than other factors. No battle has been lost since my arrival due to the lack of ammunition or equipment. [The Guomindang's] debacles in my opinion can all be attributed to the world's worst leadership." Chiang was sent $125 million, to use as he pleased, but no weapons.

The end came swiftly. At the battle of the Huai River basin, in east-central China, from September 1948 to January 1949, Chiang lost all 66 of the divisions — about 550,000 men — he committed to the fighting. Almost 330,000 of the men surrendered. The Communist victory opened the road to Nanjing, which Chiang had again made his capital at the end of World War II. With the fall of Tianjin and then Beijing in January 1949, Chiang resigned all his positions and returned briefly to his childhood village of Chikou. Recognizing that defeat was inevitable, he had 300,000 troops and most of the navy and air force transported to the island of Taiwan, off Fujian province, then raided the national treasury and transferred the entire gold reserve to Taipei, Taiwan's largest city.

In final negotiations with the Communists in April, the Guomindang representatives proposed that their government be allowed to retain control of China south of the Changjiang. The Communists demanded in response what amounted to unconditional surrender, whereupon the entire Guomindang delegation defected to the Communists. The Red Army marched into Nanjing on April 24. While the Red Army besieged Shanghai in May, Chiang was setting up house in Tsaoshan, eight miles north of Taipei. Shanghai capitulated May 25. In July Chiang returned to the mainland and at Guangzhou promised unwavering resistance to the Communists. From now on he would be solely a military man, he said, taking the battle to the CCP, and would not concern himself with politics or government. On October 1, Mao Zedong, speaking from the famed Gate of Heavenly Peace in Beijing's Forbidden City, proclaimed the establishment of the People's Republic of China. In December Chiang decamped for Taipei, with his wife, sons Ching-kuo and Wei-kuo, 800,000 troops, and 2 million followers in tow.

Fearing retribution by the victorious Communists, hundreds of thousands of Guomindang supporters fled before the Red Army's advance. Guomindang soldiers and their families rode on top of this packed train in their haste to escape Nanjing in the spring of 1949.

8

Shaking a Fist at the Mainland

Taiwan is the name of both a province of China and the main island of that province. The main island is 240 miles long, 88 miles wide, and 80 to 125 miles from the mainland across the Taiwan Straits. The province consists of the main island and 14 other islands in the main group, 64 smaller islands in the Taiwan Straits often referred to as the Pescadores, and the islands of Quemoy and Matsu, almost immediately off the Chinese coast. The main island is also known as Formosa, from *Ilha Formosa*, or "Beautiful Island," which is what the Portuguese explorers who arrived there in 1590 dubbed it. The island of Taiwan is mountainous and heavily forested. When Chiang and the 2 million refugees from the mainland arrived at the end of 1949 it had a population of about 6.5 million.

The islanders were not particularly enthusiastic about Chiang's arrival. Unlike the rest of China, Taiwan had not come under Guomindang control until 1945, when Japan was defeated in World War II. For the 50 years prior to that it had been a Japanese possession. The Guomindang administration in Taiwan had been the same mixture of greed, cor-

> *I can see Chiang now as a pathetic man. He loved his two sons, his wife and his country—his country most. But he did not know how to be a good ruler or a good father; the pathos came in trying to do good and failing.*
> —THEODORE WHITE
> American historian

Chiang, as president of the Nationalist Chinese government-in-exile, sits beneath a portrait of Sun Yat-sen in his Taiwan office. After his defeat by the Communists, Chiang simply imposed the Guomindang governmental structure on the island province and asserted that he was still the rightful leader of all of China.

The American influence in Taiwan is illustrated by this photo of a pedicab driver passing crowds lined up to see films starring Marlon Brando and Joan Crawford. At the outset Chiang's government on Taiwan was dependent upon U.S. aid for its survival.

ruption, and repression as elsewhere in China, and in 1947 there had been violent antigovernment protests. Ten thousand demonstrators were killed before the rioting was quelled.

Chiang simply imposed the Guomindang national governmental structure intact on Taiwan. Martial law was declared, under which the president — Chiang — wielded absolute power. His son Chingkuo was installed as head of the secret police. There was no right of free speech. These measures were legitimized in the constitution Chiang provided, which referred to them as "temporary provisions effective during the period of communist rebellion." Dissenters were arrested, and in two separate incidents more than 30,000 opponents of the new regime were massacred by the army. Chiang's legitimacy was based on his assertion that the Guomindang was still the rightful national government of China. According to Chiang, the Guomindang did not merely govern Taiwan; it was the government of all China, of which Taiwan was a province, and had established its new capital at Taipei.

The distinction did little to ease the resentment of the Taiwanese, who were by and large excluded from political affairs. The national government was essentially the old Guomindang, composed almost entirely of mainland Chinese. Membership in the Guomindang was crucial to political or economic success. Advocacy of Taiwanese autonomy was officially branded treasonous, and offenders were interned in camps near Taipei or on another island. Taiwanese were allowed to hold some positions in the provincial government, but it was essentially powerless. Its governor and provincial council were appointed by Chiang, and the elected provincial assembly had advisory power only and could not draft legislation. Resentment was also fueled by cultural differences. The majority of Taiwanese were the descendants of those who had come to the islands from Guangdong and Fujian in the years before the Japanese occupation. Most spoke a variation of the regional southern dialects known as Xiamen (Amoy). Many also spoke some Japanese. The majority of the 2 million Chinese who came with

American aid helped build these shelters for displaced Chinese intellectuals on Taiwan. The arrival of 2 million refugees with the Guomindang government in 1949 taxed Taiwan's economy and resources, as did the influx of refugees from the mainland throughout the 1950s.

Nationalist soldiers gaze at the People's Republic of China from the island of Quemoy in October 1958. That year shelling of Quemoy and the nearby island of Matsu by Communist batteries on the mainland precipitated an international crisis.

Chiang spoke the northern dialect, Mandarin, which was soon made the official language. (Chiang, however, had never learned Mandarin and still spoke the regional dialect of his home province of Zhejiang.)

Unyielding defiance to the Communist government of the People's Republic of China was the basic ideology of Chiang's new regime, and achieving diplomatic recognition of the Guomindang as China's national government formed the cornerstone of his foreign policy. Truman initially showed little enthusiasm for committing further aid to Chiang, but with the invasion of South Korea by communist North Korea in June 1950 and the subsequent involvement of the People's Republic of China in support of the North gave Taiwan a new strategic importance in U.S. eyes. With U.S. troops committed to defend South Korea, Taiwan was viewed as a bulwark of anticommunism in the Far East. Truman was also willing to aid the Guomindang government in Taiwan in order to deflect criticism arising from Senator Joseph McCarthy's anticommunism crusade that his administration was "soft" on communism and had "lost" China. During the hysteria of the McCarthy era many of the State Department officers who had recommended supporting Mao's forces during World War II were accused of being communists or "fellow travellers" (sympathetic or supportive of communism), and their careers were damaged. The United States gave Taiwan an estimated $2.5 billion in military aid and $1.7 billion in economic aid during the 1950s and 1960s.

During the height of the cold war — the political and economic struggle between the noncommunist and communist nations after World War II — Chiang was able to convince many of the noncommunist nations to recognize Taiwan as the legitimate government of China. Most importantly, he managed to retain the recognition of the United Nations for his claim. All the while he proclaimed his intention to retake the mainland. He ordered periodic bombing raids on the People's Republic, and in the early 1950s Guomindang divisions carried out attacks on Chinese territory from Burma, where it was rumored that Guomindang soldiers also dominated the lucrative opium trade. Guerrillas were sometimes airdropped onto the mainland from jets supplied by the United States. Despite the extensive U.S. support, it was obvious that Chiang's government lacked the strength to retake the mainland. By the terms of the 1954 mutual security treaty signed with the United States, Chiang agreed that he would not attack the People's Republic without prior U.S. consent and agreed to allow the United States to station 10,000 troops in Taiwan in exchange for continued infusions of U.S. aid and a commitment by the U.S. Navy to patrol the Taiwan Straits. Nevertheless, Chiang continued to give

This U.S.-built jet belonging to the Guomindang air force crashed and burned after being shot down over Chinese airspace in November 1958. Chiang directed military missions against the Communist government on the mainland throughout the 1950s.

yearly speeches in which he promised the imminent return of the Guomindang to a liberated China, a ritual exercise characterized by one historian as "shaking his fist at the mainland." Tension between the two Chinas continued. In 1958 the islands of Quemoy and Matsu underwent heavy shelling as a prelude to what Mao said would be a campaign to restore all of Taiwan to the control of the People's Republic, but the mobilization by the United States of what the *New York Times* called the "the most powerful air-naval fighting force in history" brought a rapid end to the crisis.

Although Chiang never completely renounced military conquest of the mainland as a goal, in the 1950s he did concede that it would have to take a backseat to other methods of liberation. Henceforth, he announced, recovery of the mainland was to be "70 percent political and 30 percent military." Taiwan was to be developed as a "model province" whose prosperity would be the envy of the mainland and would lead to popular demand for his return. The groundwork for Taiwan's economic success had already been achieved with the comprehensive land reform program Chiang had implemented shortly after his arrival from the mainland. Taiwan was a self-sufficient food producer — primarily of rice, sweet potatoes, peanuts, and soybeans — but as on the mainland, the peasantry were mostly tenant farmers who traditionally paid one-half to three-quarters of their yearly crop in rent to absentee landlords. In May 1951 Chiang established 37.5 percent of the annual crop as a ceiling on rent, then forced absentee landlords to sell their property to the Guomindang. The government in turn sold the land to the peasants with 10-year mortgages of 25 percent of the annual crop. By 1953, 80 percent of the land was owned by those who actually worked it. The economic incentives thus afforded the peasantry, combined with modern cultivation methods introduced by the government, enabled Taiwan's agricultural production to keep pace with the enormous growth of the nation's population — from 6.5 million in 1949 to 18 million and one of the world's

highest population densities in 1980 — despite no increase in the availability of arable land.

What little industry Taiwan possessed at the time of the Guomindang takeover was government owned, but Chiang encouraged private ownership. Landowners who surrendered their property to the government were sometimes compensated with ownership of factories and other industrial enterprises. Private ownership grew from somewhere near 25 percent in the early 1950s to 78 percent in 1975, although the government retained control of the sugar, oil, petroleum, power, communications, and transportation industries. Although Taiwan lacked mineral wealth, American aid enabled rapid industrialization. At one point in the 1950s American foreign aid accounted for one-fourth of Taiwan's investment capital, but by 1965 U.S. economic assistance was no longer necessary. Taiwan exported synthetic textiles, electrical equipment, and metal products, and its average annual economic growth was 8.3 percent between 1953 and 1975. Its standard of living was the second highest in Asia, trailing only Japan.

Agriculture on Taiwan at the time of Chiang's arrival was almost as undeveloped as on the mainland. Few peasants owned their own land, and most, like these women operating an antiquated irrigation device, used manpower rather than modern machinery and implements to work their fields.

Chiang delivers the inaugural address for his fourth term as president, in 1966. He insisted until his death that the Guomindang would reestablish itself on the mainland as China's national government.

Economic prosperity did much to quiet resistance to the authoritarian nature of the Guomindang government, as did the efficiency of Chiang's secret police. Chiang was reelected president in 1954, 1960, and 1966, but no legitimate political opposition was allowed to function. The Taiwanese independence movement enjoyed periodic resurgences, but the arrest of its leaders usually succeeded in driving it back underground.

Between 1969 and 1972 the number of countries recognizing Chiang's regime as the government of China declined from 67 to 52, while those recognizing the People's Republic grew from 46 to 72. Most nations desired to retain trading relations with Taiwan, but political reality dictated that the government of the world's most populous nation could no longer be ignored. Embassies in Taipei were quietly transformed into consulates. In 1969 the United States ended its naval patrols in the Taiwan Straits. Two years later, in July 1971, U.S. president Richard Nixon announced that his national security adviser, Henry Kissinger, had been engaged in secret negotiations with Premier Zhou Enlai and had arranged for the president to meet with the mainland's leaders the following year. In October the UN General Assembly voted 76 to 35 to expel the Taiwanese delegation and seat the People's Republic of China. When Nixon visited Beijing the next year, he called Taiwan a province whose disposition was an internal Chinese matter. That year Chiang was reelected president for the final time, but age and illness had made him an invalid. For the next three years he spoke only to his wife and sons. He died on April 5, 1975, and was succeeded by his son Ching-kuo, who remained in power until his death in early 1988.

U.S. president Richard Nixon meets with Mao Zedong in Beijing, February 1972. Since 1949 the United States had recognized Chiang's regime as the legitimate government of all of China, but Nixon was convinced of the strategic and diplomatic importance of redefining the United States' relationship with the "two Chinas."

Further Reading

Barnett, A. Doak. *China on the Eve of Communist Takeover*. New York: Praeger, 1963.

Crozier, Brian. *The Man Who Lost China*. New York: Scribners, 1976.

Fairbank, John King. *Chinabound: A Fifty-Year Memoir*. New York: Harper & Row, 1982.

———. *The Great Chinese Revolution: 1800–1985*. New York: Harper & Row, 1986.

———. *The United States & China*. rev. ed. New York: Viking Press, 1964.

Fairbank, John K., Edwin O. Reischauer, and Albert M. Craig. *East Asia: The Modern Transformation*. Boston: Houghton Mifflin, 1965.

Fritz, Jean. *China's Long March: 6,000 Miles of Danger*. New York: Putnam, 1988.

Karnow, Stanley. *Mao and China: Inside China's Cultural Revolution*. New York: Penguin Books, 1984.

Lawson, Don. *The Eagle and the Dragon: The History of U.S.-China Relations*. New York: Thomas Y. Crowell, 1985.

———. *The Long March: Red China Under Chairman Mao*. New York: Thomas Y. Crowell, 1983.

Luh, Pichon P.Y. *The Early Chiang Kai-shek: A Study of His Personality and Politics*. New York: Columbia University Press, 1971.

Schurmann, Franz, and Orville Schell. *Republican China: Nationalism, War, and the Rise of Communism 1911–1949*. New York: Vintage Books, 1967.

Seagrave, Sterling. *The Soong Dynasty*. New York: Harper & Row, 1985.

Snow, Edgar. *Red Star Over China*. New York: Grove Press, 1961.

Spence, Jonathan D. *The Gate of Heavenly Peace: The Chinese and Their Revolution, 1895–1980*. New York: Penguin Books, 1982.

———. *To Change China: Western Advisers in China 1620–1960*. New York: Penguin Books, 1980.

Stilwell, Joseph W. *The Stilwell Papers*. Edited by Theodore H. White. New York: Sloane, 1948.

Tuchman, Barbara. *Stilwell and the American Experience in China 1911–45*. New York: Bantam Books, 1972.

White, Theodore H. *In Search of History*. New York: Harper & Row, 1978.

Chronology

Oct. 31, 1887	Chiang Kai-shek born in Zhejiang province, China
1906–09	Attends military school in China and Japan
1911–12	End of the Qing dynasty; Sun Yat-sen becomes provisional president of the republican government and forms Guomindang (Nationalist party)
1914–18	World War I
1916–20	Chiang commands Guomindang troops and forms alliances with Shanghai gangsters
Sept. 1923	Visits Soviet Union
Jan. 1924	Guomindang endorses cooperation with the Soviet Union and the Chinese Communists; Chiang heads new military academy at Huangpu
1925	Sun Yat-sen dies; Chiang emerges as leader of Guomindang
1926	Leads Guomindang troops on northern expedition
April 1927	Chiang's forces massacre Communists in Shanghai and other cities
Dec. 1, 1927	Chiang marries Mei-ling Soong
1928	Claims control over a united China
1930–34	Directs extermination campaigns against Chinese Communists
Sept. 1931	Japanese invade Manchuria
Oct. 1934–Oct. 1935	The Long March; Communists escape Chiang's forces and establish themselves as leaders of resistance to Japan
1936	Chiang captured by the Manchurian warlord Zhang Xueliang and held until he agrees to lead a united front with the Communists against Japan
1937–45	China at war with Japan
Jan. 1941	United front comes to an end
Dec. 1941	United States declares war on Japan; China allies itself with United States; Chiang named supreme allied commander in China-Burma-India theater of war
Aug. 1945	Japan surrenders after United States drops atomic bombs on Hiroshima and Nagasaki
1946	Civil war between the Communists and the Guomindang resumes
Oct. 1949	Guomindang defeated; Mao Zedong proclaims the establishment of the People's Republic of China
Dec. 1949	Chiang flees to Taiwan
1950–75	Serves five terms as president of Taiwan
Oct. 1972	Taiwanese delegation to United Nations unseated and replaced by representatives from the People's Republic
April 5, 1975	Chiang dies; succeeded as president by his son Ching-kuo

Index

Sean Dolan is an editor and free-lance writer residing in Mount Kisco, New York. He received his B.A. in history and literature from the State University of New York at Oswego and did graduate work in history at Columbia University. He specializes in 20th-century Chinese and Japanese history.

Arthur M. Schlesinger, jr., taught history at Harvard for many years and is currently Albert Schweitzer Professor of the Humanities at City University of New York. He is the author of numerous highly praised works in American history and has twice been awarded the Pulitzer Prize. He served in the White House as special assistant to Presidents Kennedy and Johnson.

PICTURE CREDITS